Praise for Flann O'Brien (Myles na Gopaleen)

"Humourous, satirical, learned, grave-faced, crazy writing. . . . Myles was feared as were some of the ancient Gaelic poets, who it was said could kill with satire. There was no malice in him, but he could set the town laughing, and a pity for you if the laughter was at your expense."
—Benedict Kiely, *New York Times*

"As with Scott Fitzgerald, there is a brilliant ease in his prose, a poignant grace glimmering off every page."
—John Updike

"A man of black moods and (like Swift) of many ranks, Flann O'Brien brought the Irish tradition of verbal comedy to one of its perfections."
—Hugh Kenner

"If we don't cherish the work of Flann O'Brien we are stupid fools who don't deserve to have great men. Flann O'Brien is a very great man."
—Anthony Burgess

"There is no doubt about it: O'Brien was a spectacularly gifted comic writer with a rich and very Irish endowment for sheer, glorious language. . . . And he had the other Irish gifts—of boisterous comic invention, and of raising a long glass in order to tell a daring tale."
—*Newsweek*

D1042925

Other Books by Flann O'Brien

Novels

—

At Swim-Two-Birds
The Third Policeman
The Poor Mouth (An Béal Bocht)
The Hard Life
The Dalkey Archive

—

Collections

—

The Best of Myles
Stories and Plays
A Flann O'Brien Reader
The Hair of the Dogma
Further Cuttings from Cruiskeen Lawn
Myles Away from Dublin
Myles Before Myles

—

At War

Flann O'Brien

EDITED WITH AN INTRODUCTION BY
JOHN WYSE JACKSON

DALKEY ARCHIVE PRESS

Library of Congress Cataloging-in-Publication Data

O'Brien, Flann, 1911-1966
    At war / Flann O'Brien ; edited with an introduction by John Wyse Jackson.— 1st U.S. ed.
        p. cm.
    Columns from the Irish times, 1940-45.
    ISBN 1-56478-328-6 (alk. paper)
        1. Ireland—Civilization—20th century. 2. World War, 1939-1945—Ireland. I. Jackson,
John Wyse. II. Title.

PR6029.N56A6 2004
824'.912—dc22

                                                                    2003055445

Partially funded by grants from the Lannan Foundation and the Illinois Arts Council, a state agency.

Dalkey Archive Press books are published by the Center for Book Culture, a nonprofit organization.

www.centerforbookculture.org

Printed on permanent/durable acid-free paper and bound in the United States of America

Contents

Introduction

My first encounter with the author of this book took place over breakfast when I was about six years old. One morning, noticing my father chuckling over something in the newspaper, I asked him what was so funny. He told me that he was reading a column called 'Cruiskeen Lawn', which he said was bad Irish for 'A Full Jug'. The column had been running in the *Irish Times* since long before I was born, and it was written by a man with the peculiar name of Myles na gCopaleen. Myles was really another man in Dublin, a writer called Brian O'Nolan who was in fact a Civil Servant, and he kept yet another name for writing novels: Flann O'Brien. He was the funniest writer there was. I thought he sounded crazy.

Fifteen years later, by which time I had acquired all his books and a BA in English Literature, I found myself preaching obsessively to family and friends about O'Nolan-O'Brien-na-gCopaleen: they no doubt wondered who was the crazy one. He was, I insisted, Ireland's most important and interesting writer since James Joyce. By then I had been reading his work for years, at first preferring the 1939 novel *At Swim-Two-Birds*, and later deciding that *The Third Policeman*, a murder mystery whose scholarly narrator is in hell, was his best and funniest book (though it had so strange and disturbing an effect on me that in the end I swore never to read it again).

It had been towards the end of my school career that the rot set in in earnest. I won a Prize for Improvement and was allowed to choose a copy of *The Best of Myles*, a hilarious collection of early 'Cruiskeen Lawn' pieces which had been edited by his academic brother, Kevin, after O'Nolan's death in 1966. Three further volumes of extracts soon joined it at my bedside. With these under my belt, I began ferreting wildly through back issues of the *Irish Times* in libraries, and was rewarded with almost 3,000 more columns in tiny print – they had appeared up to six times a week for a quarter of a century. I was stunned by what I had found. 'Cruiskeen Lawn' was unique. It amounted to perhaps four million words in all, and it was, to my mind incontrovertibly, a hugely original and triumphantly sustained work of art. How could this marvel have lain there unrecognized for so long? Admittedly, some sections had been rendered almost incomprehensible by the passage of time, while others seemed at first sight to be jaded or otherwise unsatisfactory, but as a whole, it was an immense literary achievement, fully worthy of Flann O'Brien at the height of his powers. Why had 'Cruiskeen Lawn' not yet been acclaimed as the masterpiece it was, not even in Ireland? I intended to find out more about it. What were the writer's aims and motives? How, for example, had it begun?

On 4 June 1940, the day on which the last British troops were being rescued from Dunkirk, a letter from an old acquaintance of both Joseph Conrad and Swinburne was published in the *Irish Times*. It was signed F. O'Brien. Immediately afterwards, an army of pseudonymous correspondents invaded the paper to the general amusement (and bemusement) of readers. Up to nine surreal letters a day appeared over the next three months. Subjects discussed included Ibsen's problems with dandruff, the use of sewers by Ireland's artistic élite, and the dearth of hair on the legs of the Hitler Jugend. How many were written by Brian O'Nolan is now impossible to tell, but when the paper's decidedly eccentric editor, R. M. Smyllie (who had himself contributed to the 'controversy' under the name of 'The O'Madan') met O'Nolan, he asked him to stop writing letters and to contribute a regular article instead. It was to be in the Irish language, and he would get paid for it. The column began at once, on 28 September.

'Cruiskeen Lawn' was soon appearing almost every day, and at first *was* in Irish. It was scurrilous, highly inventive, and almost untranslatable. Nothing like it had ever been perpetrated in the language. Then on October 19th Myles wrote in English for the first time – an extract opens this book. He was soon interrupting his virtuous flow of Irish quite often, generally with unlikely anecdotes about the poets Keats and Chapman. From September 1941 the languages alternated daily for two years; thereafter, columns in Irish were rare. Apart from *An Béal Bocht*, which grew from the Irish half of 'Cruiskeen Lawn', he would write no other novels until 1960.

There was, of course, a world war going on when 'Cruiskeen Lawn' began. Neutral Ireland, being powerless in relation to the cataclysmic events taking place overseas, became a state in neutral, virtually isolated from the rest of mankind. Though there were shortages of commodities such as petrol, coal and tobacco, the war (which the authorities dealt with by calling it an 'Emergency') somehow seemed to be very far away. The question of neutrality, however, sparked heated debate, particularly among old 'Ascendancy' readers of the *Irish Times* whose emotional links with Britain were still close.

There were protests when, like a Hibernian cuckoo, 'Cruiskeen Lawn' appeared beside the editor's hallowed leading articles, where Smyllie evaded the Censor by cheering on the allies as neutrally as he could – or as Myles put it, 'played with his Panzerdivisionen'. One angry reader accused Myles of 'holding a party when the house next door was burning down.' Smyllie, though he spoke no Irish himself, felt that the new column would help to assert the Irishness of the *Irish Times* and might attract a new sort of reader – sorely needed as the state's Protestant population was rapidly dwindling. Within a short time 'Cruiskeen Lawn' had become yet another of Dublin's great unnatural phenomena, like Nelson's Pillar or *Ulysses* or the dark hoppy air around the brewery at St James' Gate.

When Myles appeared in English almost everybody who read the *Irish Times* read him. They did so because he usually gave you a good laugh. (Later he would also be read for the virulence of his invective.) There were always those who followed the column because its intellectual content could be flattering if you understood it – Myles sometimes wrote in Latin, German or French, and in his more meditative pieces his vocabulary in English was often a challenge. The paper was now being taken by educated parties from Dublin's business, professional and academic classes, and it was for these, the new Irish intelligensia, that Myles chiefly wrote. These readers (who were mostly men) would stay with him for the span of a generation, effortlessly absorbing his idiosyncratic social and cultural analysis of their country. Like a funfair mirror, 'Cruiskeen Lawn' reflected their own beliefs and preconceptions back at them, with boundaries distorted and certainties doubtful. These men would be pivotal figures in the development of the new Ireland, politicians and lecturers, doctors and lawyers, writers and businessmen, Jesuits. These were the men who laid the foundations of the shining Utopia we have today.

To lead such people, as Myles did again and again, into the alien and trackless territories of his mind was no petty accomplishment. And, despite any initial objections to Smyllie's 'hired humorist', many of the more traditional *Irish Times* readers, 'no petty people' themselves, also became faithful readers. Myles's independence of thought, his respect for education and the classics, his contempt for nationalistic flag-waving, his scorn for the 'backwardness' of the country (and of those who were supposed to be running it), all gave sustenance to those who weren't quite sure how welcome they were any more in this new Ireland. He usually gave them a good laugh as well.

As my obsession grew and I began to think more deeply about the unique literary treasure that I believed I had unearthed, I came to realise that the published collections so far, sparkling though they were, failed to convey several vital aspects of 'Cruiskeen Lawn'. This was inevitable: no book recognisable as such could hope to contain the column's scale, cumulative effect or unpredictability. Though *The Best of Myles*, for example, had chapters that were loosely thematic, the original reader opening his morning paper had no idea whether Myles was going to amuse, anger, surprise, disgust or bore him. Accordingly, when preparing this volume, my first decision was to preserve the order of original publication (and dates are given at the back of the book). Such a chronological arrangement would restore something of Myles's unpredictability. It would also make it for the first time possible to track the trajectory of the mercurial and troubled mind of Myles na gCopaleen, on its travels through time.

Knowing whether *this* was said before *that* reveals something of the underlying structure of 'Cruiskeen Lawn'. The column has generally been dismissed as a series of humorous squibs, satires and sketches, albeit displayed against a glittering backdrop of verbal prestidigitation. Brilliant, perhaps, but not, finally, 'important'. However, as I studied it more closely, I gradually discerned a work that was far more challenging than even I had suspected. Here was surely one of the great monuments of the century, a modernist (or rather a proleptically postmodernist) *coup de maître*, written in two primary and several secondary languages whose boundaries are repeatedly breached and confused. I began to think of 'Cruiskeen Lawn' as some unidentified subspecies of the fiction family, a random, episodic, wildly innovative rough beast of a 'novel', in which the novel form itself has been stretched to screaming point and beyond.

* * *

O'Nolan appropriated his columnist's name from 'Myles na Copaleen', a horse-dealer in Dion Boucicault's 1860 melodrama, *The Colleen Bawn*. This stage-Irish rogue and 'character' sings the song 'Cruiskeen Lawn' in the play (and his other song is 'Brian O'Linn', which in its Irish version can be inverted to form 'Flann O'Brien'). But the new Myles na gCopaleen was not just another pseudonym: he would become the greatest fictional artefact that O'Nolan ever created. Myles may be the 'writer' of

'Cruiskeen Lawn', but he is also the main actor in it. He is a volatile and moody creature: he can be puckish, witty, irreverent, or simply childish, and he can be petulant, obsessive, brutal, even desperate. There is something approaching the tragic about him. Much given to hiding behind the truth, he is rarely without a mask. Myles frequently (perhaps invariably) appoints surrogates to speak for him, leaving the reader always in doubt as to his current level of irony or detachment. He may write as Dublin gurrier or European aristocrat, inventor or thief, scholar, journalist, cheap comic, classicist, misogynist, diplomat, grammarian, family doctor, philosopher, prophet, potential suicide, madman, critic or god. Who the Myles behind them all actually is remains a mystery.

In this book, some of Myles's 'surrogates' will already be familiar to those who know the previously published collections: the jovial Dublin man whose life revolves around the activities of his self-opinionated brother, the pedagogue obsessed by clichés, and (acting as Myles's foils) the brain-dead and infinitely shockable 'Plain People of Ireland'. There are also new encounters with Keats and Chapman, those unlikely friends who inhabit an alternative world governed not by the laws of time and causality but by the absolute necessity for final ambiguity, a world in which the miserable end always justifies the means. Yet, Myles na gCopaleen is not Everyman, and underlying the various voices in 'Cruiskeen Lawn' there is continuity and fictional progress: the savant's personality, protean and deeply complex as it is, matures and metamorphoses as time goes by. During the years covered in these pages, 1940 to 1945, it darkens alarmingly.

During this time Brian O'Nolan wrote a story called 'Two in One'. A taxidermist's assistant murders his despotic employer, and in an effort to conceal his evil deed inadvertently traps himself inside the flayed skin of the dead taxidermist. When the police come snooping, he cannot explain where he himself has vanished to, and is arrested for his own murder. Something of the sort was happening to O'Nolan too in Dublin: though he was careful as a Civil Servant never officially to admit responsibility for the column, he was now being addressed by his friends, almost to a man, as 'Myles'. In the eyes of the world Brian O'Nolan was turning into his own creation.

Whether or not O'Nolan's perception of himself was also becoming entangled with the character he had invented, it was essential for his own well-being that the phenomenon be resisted. But how better to resist it than by appearing to go along with it? Using the sharpest weapons available to the Irish writer, silence and cunning, the 'real' Brian O'Nolan went into a sort of internal exile, rendering himself virtually 'unknowable' to all but a very few. From this he would never fully emerge again.

Naturally, there were repercussions on his life, and on the contents of the 'Cruiskeen Lawn'. Although it remained what it was always meant to be, a humorous column, and poured out plenty of the mixture much as before, increasingly its targets included Myles himself. The prose of this period is as strong as anything Flann O'Brien ever achieved, a disguised voice reciting the confusing story of a hidden life. As to an extent is also the case with James Joyce, Brian O'Nolan's ambiguous personal identification with his 'narrator' means that Myles na gCopaleen may or may not be taken by the reader as a wholly autonomous fictional character. This gives rise to profound metafictional implications which I do not feel inclined to go into here, except to say that it turns 'Cruiskeen Lawn' into a many-layered literary conundrum, and one that is as impressive in execution as it is in scale.

As mentioned, the words 'Cruiskeen Lawn' are usually translated as 'The Full Little Jug', or for some reason, 'The Overflowing Little Jug'. It is a phrase used in Irish drinking songs, where the size of the jug is much less relevant than the contents, which are whiskey, or perhaps poteen. Alcohol was an undeniable factor in O'Nolan's creative processes: its use (and abuse) underlies a good deal of the column. I have been reliably informed that some submissions were written when he was very drunk, though I cannot identify any of them in print. The subject of drink crops up frequently, but that of alcoholism is barely mentioned: life for a normal man, particularly in Dublin, is assumed to involve much heavy drinking. At times, Myles's writing seems to glisten with a painful, hungover quality that scarcely conceals fear and desperation just below the surface. The laughter becomes bitter, black, ironic, the flights of fantasy almost manic. In these revealing columns (some of them reprinted here), which read like extracts from the diary of a depressive megalomaniac, Myles both expresses and embodies helplessness in the face of the banality, agony and tedium of his life.

Let it not be forgotten that Myles na gCopaleen remains a fictional character. How autobiographical these disturbing pieces actually are is still a question. But it is a fact that even before O'Nolan lost his job in the Civil Service in the early 1950s, his natural habitat, in and out of office hours, was the pub. He was no Brendan Behan, however. Neither raconteur nor singer, his usual drinking accessories were a hat, a newspaper and a gloomy silence, broken only by the occasional observation. He often drank alone, and rarely seemed happy. In later years, jobless and mercifully carless, he could sometimes be seen in Dublin in the late afternoons, making his unsteady way towards the bungalow in Stillorgan that he shared with Evelyn, his wife – there were to be no children. An acquaintance observed him one day advancing hand over hand in a southerly direction along the supportive railings of Merrion Square. He was repeating over and over to himself the words, 'Fuck the fucking fuckers.'

Who these particular fuckers were we shall never know. When he was in the mood for battle, O'Nolan's anger had many targets, and Myles na gCopaleen was only too glad to express it for him. Of the Irish Civil Service – and of the Government that was civilly served by it – Myles repeatedly asserted that both were staffed by farmers' sons ('turnip-snaggers') with a thin veneer of education over their innate, ignorant rurality, and by Corkmen. Dublin Corporation was given periodic roastings from what he called his 'roastrum'. The old 'Ascendancy' were mocked for their deluded view of history, their baseless Anglophilia, and their paternalistic and patronising attitude to the young Irish state. The country's architects, lawyers, musicians, bankers and scholars, as well as its artists, poets and aesthetes (or 'corduroys') were heartily sneered at for their manifold pretensions.

Even the highminded Institute for Advanced Studies (recently founded by Eamon De Valera) had its academic leg strenuously pulled in various directions, and was parodied by Myles's 'Research Bureau'. The Irish Tourist Board, the Electricity Supply Board and other national services came under vicious attack for inefficiency or worse. Myles always pilloried the use of jaded and ungrammatical English (and Irish), eagerly parading examples of bad writing to demonstrate the essential incapacity of the perpetrator and hence the worthlessness of all his opinions. Although O'Nolan himself was devoted to the first national language as a scholastic discipline and a civilized accomplishment, he was equally savage in his onslaughts on the revivalists with their dreams of a monoglot Ireland in which chaste Gaelic colleens would dance chaste Gaelic dances at crossroads that were signposted in the chaste Gaelic tongue. Not even his employer, the editor of the *Irish Times*, was spared.

Perhaps the most virulent of Brian O'Nolan's dislikes, however, was the all-purpose liberal, and here the short story writer Sean O'Faolain regularly bore the brunt. In 1940 O'Faolain had founded the *Bell*, a monthly magazine that aimed to reflect the real attitudes and concerns of Irish society, to define the place of the artist within it, and to fight censorship. At a time when Ireland's morals were being stringently policed by both the Roman Catholic Church and the Censorship Board, Myles mercilessly attacked and lampooned such members of Ireland's literary set, writers who mouthed platitudes about how disgraceful it was that their works of 'literature' should be banned in their own country. He accused them of reaping publicity, acclaim and a fraudulent moral superiority from the unfounded notoriety of their books. If he had been empowered to do so, he would have banned them himself (though on grounds of literary incompetence). Later he was to tell a correspondent that he hoped *The Hard Life*, his 1961 novel, *would* be banned, earning him the kudos (and sales) enjoyed by such as Frank O'Connor, Kate O'Brien, and O'Faolain himself. Alas, as it turned out, *The Hard Life* failed to catch the censor's by then dimming eye.

Some years ago, while gathering together a previous selection of Brian O'Nolan's earliest writings (*Myles Before Myles*), I found myself drinking whiskey in his sitting room in Stillorgan at three o'clock in the afternoon. Pouring it, but consuming none herself, was his widow, Evelyn, who had kindly agreed to see me. She seemed to imagine that I had an infinite capacity for alcohol at that hour, for she filled my glass half-full of neat whiskey and, when I automatically drank it, kept repeating the dose whenever I wasn't looking. By the time several lengthy bouts of small-talk were over, I had forgotten most of the things I had intended to ask her about. Instead, it was she who was asking me questions, about people in Dublin literary circles and if I trusted any of them or not. As I had never met many of these giants, I said that I had never trusted any of them with anything. She told me that her husband had never trusted them either.

As far as I can recall, though she clearly had her opinions, Mrs O'Nolan did not want to say much about either her late husband or his writings. My queries about the past elicited only sad but indeterminate reflections on his problems with money and on other unfortunate occurrences too tedious for her to go back over in detail. At the mention of financial difficulties in the 1950s, I roused myself to inquire why her husband pretended to have lost the only manuscript of his greatest novel, *The Third Policeman* (written in 1939 but turned down as 'too fantastic' by his English publisher, Longmans). I knew that soon after his death she had taken it out of its drawer and sent it off for publication. She replied quietly that she hadn't liked to worry Brian by mentioning it. 'If he was sober it would have only upset him and if he had drink taken he would have told me to puff off.' Then she remembered that he had once said something about

16

needing to recast the book in the third person. *The Third Policeman* in the third person! Inconceivable. Perhaps it was a joke. I staggered off a few minutes later to look for a bus, knowing that I would never understand Brian O'Nolan.

John Wyse Jackson,
London, June 1999

Editorial Note

Readers may reasonably wonder how the choices for this novel draught from 'Cruiskeen Lawn' were made. It was very simple: confining myself loosely to the 'war' years for reasons of space, I picked out the pieces in English that I found most interesting and enjoyable, and checked that none had been previously republished in book form. Then, keeping their order, I read the story they told, divided it for convenience into chapters, and passed it to Hector McDonnell for illustration. The chapter titles and preambles are my own, and may safely be ignored as an intrusive editor's indulgence. Flann O'Brien's *At War* is just one person's journey through part of Myles na gCopaleen's unique four million word continuum. Feel free to make your own.

Taken in its entirety as a sustained literary creation, the writer's pseudonymous masterwork called 'Cruiskeen Lawn' might reasonably have borne the title: 'The Golden Hours of Myles na gCopaleen.' This is the sage's holy book of Byzantium.

Le Fournier, 'The Fate of the Codex', in *True Believer: A Festschrift for Otto Kraus*, ed. Henderson & du Garbandier, Lille, 1966.

1
The Shy Child

In which Myles na gCopaleen embarks on his ministry with the tale of the sad fate of another prodigiously gifted Renaissance Man. Vital questions concerning aesthetics and the indigenous drama must be answered before the savant can present his war-weary people with important new proposals to ameliorate the tribulations of life on their island. It may still be possible modestly to celebrate the publication of an historic volume in the Irish tongue (and to wish all a festive Christmas) but, for the nation which speaks that noble tongue, Myles has ominous fraternal prognostications to report.

i

Spring is lurking like a shy child in the smiling parkland. Not yet has she decked the empty trees with ferny shoot or showered with dainty bloom the plum-tree wild. But those who listen can hear the rustle of her silken gown and notice on the wind her first sweet whisper. Soon the daffodils will come, marching like a band of haloed angels on the upland lawn.

If some people are allowed to write like that, there is no reason why everybody should not do it, and if it makes the plum-tree wild, it can't be helped. But there must be some mistake. It is either the wrong paragraph, the wrong paper, the wrong season or the wrong hemisphere.

ii

I notice that the current issue of *Irish Travel* is adorned with the Irish supertitle *Cuaird Faoi Éirinn*. So far as my knowledge goes, this means nothing more or less than 'Travel Under Ireland'. The suggestion seems to be that the Irish Tourist Authority is taking note of the times we live in and is arranging underground tours for scared visitors. Such enterprise deserves (and gets herewith) unqualified commendation.

I cannot dismiss from my mind the picture of a group of bright-faced Americans being carefully lowered through a man-hole or excavation in O'Connell street and emerging on to some quiet thoroughfare in Waterford –

Voices: This stuff is supposed to be in Irish. Why English – and on this day of all others? What in the name of heaven is the idea?

Mise: There is a reason for everything.

Voices: Well?

Mise: You will find a nice leading article in Irish (and *on* Irish) in every other newspaper in the land on St. Patrick's Day. This is known as saving-the-language. Throughout the whole year they print nothing but offensive puerilities in Irish, but they make up for it all by this annual leader.

Voices (doubtful, but half-convinced): I see. Perhaps you will explain what you mean by 'offensive puerilities'?

Mise (in a patient tired voice): Certainly. The Gael wakes up in the morning and grabs his favourite newspaper. Vast letters on the news page inform him that (say) Bardia has been captured by the British. He souses himself in this event to the tune of three columns, and then turns the page wearily in search of some smooth emollient Gaelic. After a lot of poking in the paper's backyard, he finds something like this:–

The intelligence has been made naked that the city Bardia has been invaded by Saxons this Tuesday that went past.

The astonished Gael then realises that he is regarded as a cretin.

Voices (impressed): I see. And these leading articles you speak of . . .

Mise: They are nauseating. The language itself, having been ridiculed for a year, is beslobbered with laudatory mucus. Then there are usually a few crocodile spasms about the sea-divided Gael, the four green fields, the-friends-we-know-are-by-our-side-and-the-foes-we-hate-before-us – all the claptrap that has made fortunes for cute professional Irishmen in America.

Voices (disturbed, but with a note of forced cheerfulness): That sounds very bad, indeed, but –

Mise (savagely): The whole thing is an outrage, a scandal that cries to heaven. To write a word of Irish today would be to run the risk of being grouped with –

Voices (hastily): But is this all we're going to have – a tirade, violent denunciations, intemperate language? Surely, that is recognised everywhere as the height of vulgarity? We have far too much of that sort of thing in this country. What we want is a little sympathy, a spirit of give-and-take, a readiness to pull together and forgive each others' failings, a realisation of our common humanity –

Mise (bitterly): – a sense of humour, a desire to see the other fellow's point of view, charity in the heart rather than on the tongue, a genuine desire to help, proficiency in table-tennis, six times a week to the pictures, a longing to be curled up with a good book, a tennis-club hop on Saturday night. What would you like now?

Voices (with nauseating cheerfulness): If we could have a few good jokes . . .

Mise: Very well. Let me get back to the tourist question. Visitors often comment on the fine men who handle their travel and customs difficulties on the landing-stage in Dun Laoghaire. They are described as witty, courteous, helpful, frightfully Irish, and even funny.

Voices: Well?

Mise: But to me they will always be stage Irishmen.

Voices (meditatively, admiringly): How on earth does he think of them?

iii

To the dentist on Wednesday. Previously he had suggested on the telephone that 'it would be no harm to let us have a squint at it,' 'have a general look round,' 'fix you up in a jiffy,' and so on. This sounded like the encouragement one might expect from a good-natured hangman. It was, in fact, nothing more or less. The terrifying and bloody experience which followed my encasement in evil-smelling rubber aprons will not be recounted here. Suffice it to say that blood and sweat, toil and tears were offered in abundance by the two ghouls who were in charge. In my conscious moments these torments were augmented by unasked for monologues; politics, polite learning and the strangeness of the times were observed to flower in many a lonely phrase.

The Truth About Teeth

All this is by the way, as a corduroys* would probably murmur. What I want to emphasise is that in the art of dentistry we have a permanent threat to the integrity, harmony and indivisibility of the human entity. One has only to recall momentarily the works of Aristophanes to realise it. It is quite wrong to think, much less to talk, about a tooth being 'extracted'. The operation is by no means so simple. On the contrary, here we have complexity that embraces the human, terrestrial and occult continua. In reality the whole body is amputated from the tooth. The operation is thus as major as may be. Where a living person is deprived by gas or drugs of self-competence and consciousness and then divided into two parts by means of steel instruments (as happens in a simple 'extraction'), it will be evident that there has been violent and irrevocable interference with the personal integrity of the patient and thus proportionately with the balance of the entire universe, of which he is for himself the sole perceptor, sensuant and interpreter. Always remember that life and living is simply a relationship between the cosmos and the human cosmiculate. Impair the integrity of the latter and you have unbalance and partial invalidity. If you are subjected to anaesthesia and parted permanently from an essential molar, the consciousness that you re-attain is by no means identical with that enjoyed before, inasmuch as you have been made incomplete, left with a diminished capacity for nervous excitation and cognition, reduced even in weight. The minutiae of the physical world impinge on a deficient consciousness, causing an inferior reaction. Look up your Aristophanes on that too, and, provided you have the time, have a go also at your Aristotle.

Massimiliano Sforzi

All this is also by the way. My real point is that today we celebrate the fifth centenary of Massimiliano Sforzi, Florentine doyen of mediaeval dentists. Crony of da Vinci and Michelangelo, confidant of Cellini, sewer-architect to Lorenzo de Medici, he was engineer, ball-maker, fiddler, sewer-consultant, painter, fencer, sculptor, dentist, barber, surgeon, herbalist, bon-vivant, pioneer of arterial drainage, tenor, boxer, and anything else you like to think of. He invented, perfected, and brought to the grave with him, an extraordinary science which enabled him to remove teeth, repair them, *and put them back again!* The old records show that the process was quite painless, and that the replaced teeth were reseated in the gums with a precision that would deceive the eye.

It was useless to go to Sforzi and complain of a simple toothache. The whole lot would have to come out, and they would be put back only when every defect, however invisible and unsuspected, had been detected and remedied. The better-class orders had all their teeth extracted annually for cleaning, as a matter of good breeding and hygiene – some cranks even weekly. People who were eccentric about animals brought their horses, dogs and cats for periodic dedentalling at the old workshops in the Piazza dello Pidocchio, and parted with savage fees without a thought. Whether one were a lady, a libertine or a bay gelding, to be seen occasionally *edentato* for a day was the recognised mark of high birth.

A Contretemps

The records recount a queer affair that occurred towards the end of the master's life. He had spent a busy day in his *chirurgia*. By evening he had removed from man and beast a total of some 2,000 fangs, each separate mouthful being arranged in numbered trays on a vast table. He then repaired for the week-end to the villa of friend Lorenzo, where, it seems, Michelangelo and da Vinci had arranged a four. On the Sunday the slatternly *caseria*, very much the worse for wine, entered the surgery and embarked on drunken sweeping operations. What happened may well be imagined. Over went the tooth-table, and down on the dirty floor fell the teeth like a shower of heavy hail. Seeing what she had done, the slut took fright and summoned her husband and sons. The four set to work, and after several hours had the trays back on the table, with a fair selection of teeth in each. Your true Florentine will still relate the sequel as if it had happened only the other day. Versions may differ, but the same absurd dénouement is found in each. Very strange things were seen the next day. A dancing girl from the follies, saluting an elderly general, was astonished to find her own dazzling ivories flashing back at her bewitchingly from under the martial moustaches. A matinée idol unwittingly confronted his admirers with a mouthful of flat yellow oblongs which had evidently in their time champed countless feeds of straw. A high-born horse-fancier, opening the jaws of a spirited Arab to assess its age, was astonished to encounter the unmistakable snarl of his wealthy aunt.

Old Sforzi tried to pass the thing off as something of a joke, but on his head fell many a curse, distortedly uttered through alien teeth. He died soon afterwards, some say of a broken heart.

*corduroys: Aesthete, verse-speaker or other member of the bearded class; from the legwear characteristically worn by same.

iv

I had a reference recently to the distinguished Corkman, Marshal Tim O'Shenko*, who has attained to a position of eminence in the Red Army, and who bears with him the best wishes of every right-thinking Irishman in his handling of the difficult tasks with which he has been faced. In the *Evening Mail* of the 31st July I found mention made of another commander called 'Tomoshenko'. Tom, of course, would be the brother. I met him many years ago in the South, and remember him as a good fellow and a good sportsman. He was of burly build and bore himself with that charm and shyness which one finds only in big men. He received his schooling, I think, at Rockwell, and played full-back for Garryowen in 1924-25. Unless I am much mis-

taken, he went on for teaching and took his B.A. at National†
where he was a prominent exponent of socialistic doctrines at
the gatherings of the Literary and Historical Society. It is,
indeed, a far cry from National to the wastes of Soviet Russia.
Quae regio in Earlsfort Terrace nostri non plena laboris?‡

A Letter from the Interior

Tom took a pardonable pride in the work of his better-known
brother. I think the last time I laid eyes on him was at Lahinch
in 1934, where he had been recuperating from an illness and
putting in some golf. He seemed despondent, and refused to be
cheered up by rather back-slapping exuberance.

'I've had a letter from Tim,' he said, 'and he takes a very poor
view of what is happening in Germany. He says that there will
be a world war in seven years, if not sooner. He has joined the
Red Army as a private.'

'Well, well, well,' I said. I was genuinely surprised at this rather
idealistic move on the part of Tim, whom I had always heard of
as a hard-headed business type. I knew that he had made plenty
of money operating some suet cartel east of the Urals.

'I think I will be going away soon myself,' Tom said. 'After all,
when one's brother is out there . . . .'

That, I thought, was big-hearted Tom all over. He is out there
now, and in the thick of things. One does not take sides in these
neutral latitudes, but I think most of my readers will join me in
expressing the hope that we will yet see both Tom and Tim
O'Shenko back in Ireland safe and sound, matching their military wit against General Bogey on the Hermitage terrain, and
fighting with the same indomitable will to win. Ireland never
had two more likeable sons.

---

*Marshal Timoshenko (1895-1970) who successfully defended Moscow
from the Wehrmacht in 1941.

†The National University of Ireland, at University College, Earlsfort
Terrace, Dublin.

‡From Virgil's *Aeneid* (I.459-60): . . .*quae regio in terris nostri non plena
laboris?* (Is there a part of the world that is not full of our activities?)

iv

Advanced Studies Corner

Though paid not a tithe of the number of Mickey O'Bolgers pulled down annually by our University know-alls, my researches into the Irish language and antiquities continue unabated. My more recent studies enable me to reveal the real name of Willy Reilly's Colleen Bawn. 'Bawn' stands for 'White', and not 'Phair', as Wechselmann has hazarded in the *Zeitschrift für Celtische Philologie*. As to the other name, the Irish word *coll* means 'hazel', and is here used with the diminutive affix '-een' or 'ín' as a device of endearment. Her name was therefore Hazel White (or Hazeleen White), and she was probably one of the Whites of West Kerry. 'Colleen' is also the Irish for the surname Hazlitt. The gentle Elia, William Hazlitt, would be known in Ireland as Liam MacColleen, though, admittedly, it is a bit late in the day to be saying so.

v

Home Hints

Be sure to cut this out, paste it on cardboard, and hang it up in a prominent position in the kitchen. My illustration explains what the Gas Company, the Electricity Supply Board and the Government expect you to do in these difficult times about your shaving water. In nearly every household vast saucepans of clothing or potatoes are boiled every morning. Your task, no less than your duty, is to fit the saucepan with the catchment apparatus illustrated. The water that boils over is thus neatly husbanded and deposited in the waiting mug. When the mug is full you carry on with your shaving, or make yourself a refreshing cup of cocoa if you happen to be a lady.

Foot Note Please do not write to the Editor pointing out that William Hazlitt was not Elia. He probably knows.

vi

Old Times at the Abbey

A point that should be carefully observed was to allow characters – where they had to do so – time enough off stage to change dresses.
　– Mr Lennox Robinson, lecturing on 'Making a Play'.

I agree absolutely. I remember making a mess of this important matter in a play of mine that was done in the early days of the Abbey. The hero, a weedy clerk who was meant to show more and more lion-heart as his physique deteriorated, was required by the plot to appear in eight different suits of clothes. The headlong tempo of my stuff, however, allowed him only a few seconds for each change. The unfortunate man (a trier if there ever was one) had no choice but to pull the second suit on over the first one, the third over the first two, and so on. The result may be imagined. Instead of withering away as he was meant to, he was considerably larger at each entrance and grew in the course of an hour into a gross, puffy Colossus of a man, lathered in sweat and as irritable as a bag of cats. His appearance in pyjamas in the last act is still remembered by the older Abbey-goers. The reinforcement of eight pairs of trousers made it impossible to sit down or bend his legs, and he had to lumber about the stage like an enormous stiff-legged Boris Karloff, trying vainly to jerk his sweaty hands out of his eight-ply sleeves. He looked as delicate and as aesthetic as a jack-elephant after eating a whole kraal of natives. The accumulations of waistcoat and surcoat on the actor's tiny chest put a strain on his heart, and he died (in poverty, incidentally) two years later. The play was ruined and Willie Fay* was furious.

*William Fay (1872-1947) was, with W B Yeats and others, a founder of the Abbey Theatre, Dublin.

vii

A thing that is worth trying is the following. Get a rather romanticised photograph of yourself, with plenty of hair on view, and the whole picture slightly out of focus. Stain it yellow with weak tea, and get it put into an austere narrow-edged frame. Then make your way to the Abbey Theatre, with the thing under your coat. Hob-nob in the foyer with the riff-raff you will meet there on a first night, however much you dislike the row that is made by the overpaid talking drayma to the underworked. Ignore the fine lumps of women, and keep your mind on business. Praise everything and everybody, but be cautious if you meet a quondam Abbey author, because he is there to put in a night's sneering at the piece on hands. Make yourself popular. Buy coffee for strangers, and save women from being killed in the savage exodus for drinks at half-time. If you see the author of the play looking for 'your real opinion', give him lie after lie until his gills bloom like the 'Stop' on traffic lights.

Then –

After the last curtain, break your way into the dressing rooms, still blathering out of you like a lost sheep. When you get a suitable opportunity, sneak up into the Green Room and fix your picture on the wall in the middle of all the others. Then go home and rest content.

Some fine day there will be a little party in the Green Room.

'And who is this?' a visitor will say. Nobody will admit that he doesn't know. 'Willie Fay to the life', somebody will say. 'Surely you remember Seumas O'Kelly?' 'That's James Stephens as a young man.' 'That's Martyn.' Possibly some observant ass will mutter something about 'that cattle-jobber that's always hanging about below'; but he will be ignored by the know-alls and refused a second cup of tea.

The whole point of the thing is that nobody will have the courage to take the picture down. Immortality is easier to win in Dublin than a reasonably priced room that is bright, clean and free from beetles.

viii

People who do not live in Dublin (or, living there, keep clear of the 'intellectual' rat-runs) would find it very hard to credit the extraordinary guff that passes for enlightened conversation when a couple of beards and corduroys get together. It is very funny. It is so good that it should be recorded. In fact, it *is* being recorded – by me and my stool-pigeons. Today I inaugurate a feature unique in the annals of Irish journalism. I print below one of the best of these spiels that has come to my notice. With it I give the reader my categorical assurance that it is genuine. It has not been added to or altered in any way; the words are given exactly as they were spoken. Stand clear!

'I remember when we thrilled in retrospect to the bizarre adventure of quattrocento ballistics and thought of Leonardo as the spiritual father of Nobel and Maginot! But for me there is nothing in the whole history of quattrocento, cinquecento, nor even in the late horror of the seicento so terribly exciting as those charming words of Pontus de Thiard: "Houura! Cornes-au-cul! Vive al Père Ubu!" In France still beats the fervent heart of humanism, and no pigment from the palette of Georges Braque could fail to excite the palate of Rabelais or Montaigne. Then you get that gigantic efflorescence of tectonic virtuosity round the Île de France – I can still recall the ecstasy in which I first saw the west façade of the glorious little Church of Saint Dagobert sans Culotte (corner of the Rue des Grues Nues); there the joyful old masons had so done their work, each stone fitted into its neighbour so exquisitely, each quoin worked so independently, so proudly, yet with such true Gallic sympathy, such Anglo-Saxon collaboration that (irresistibly reminded of Vlacsz' 'Waterworks' quintet) (Bé-mol, No. B36, 'L,' '41) I cried out: "See! They are singing! Singing! Singing!'"

Now!

If any reader can recall ever having heard anything to beat that, let him or her write to me and tell me. Such things should not be kept in secret for selfish pleasure. It is no use, however, inventing speeches that were never said, becase a child could tell the genuine article from any concocted substitute. This is the sort of thing that just can't be faked. The real thing rings like a silver bell and shines like gold.

I showed the gem above to a butty of mine. His comment was: '*Éist le glór na h-óinsighe agus gheobhair Braque!*'* Those who have sufficient education to understand will admit that this is neat.

---

*Listen to the voice of the fool and you will get Braque! The Irish proverb is *Éist le glór na habhann agus gheobhair breac*. (Listen to the sound of the river and you will get fish.)

ix

Several correspondents have written to me inquiring what are the prospects that cement fishing rods may be made available during the emergency to eke out diminishing supplies of the genuine article. My answer is that the position is difficult, but not hopeless. Cement I cannot promise, but a cartel composed of immigrants – landless men without a country – is working night and day to produce a rod made from pressed slack. I have been privileged to see a few specimens, and I can assure my readers that they are by no means bad. True, one requires gloves in handling them, and the tensile quality is not pronounced.

Nevertheless, they have their utility and their own austere beauty. They are admirable for yanking typhoid-sodden roach from the metal bellies of our furred canals.

Another company is experimenting with a new type of ersatz salmon rod. The two lower sections are made from pressed butcher's offals, while the top piece is made from a mixture of steam slack and low-grade suet, the mixture being shaped by hand, baked for four hours at a temperature of 560 degrees Fahrenheit and then electro-plated. It is quite a satisfactory article for casting, but a really big salmon in his health might fracture the suet-piece unless the angler is very experienced.

Any reader who desires further information should write to the Institute for Advanced Studies, Merrion Square.

X

Today's Illustration

This interesting wheel is peculiarly suitable for rough pot-holed roads. The steel tyre is undulated in a way that will give the vehicle a series of *uniform* bumps.

This element of periodicity reconciles the human body to what is called *anró na marcuigheachta** and has the effect, paradoxically enough, of making rough roads smooth. Try it and see.

*Literally saddle-soreness.

xi

Myself and the Theatre

Now that Mr Lennox Robinson has delivered his lectures on how to write a play, there remain only my disquisitions on how not to write a play. No person who has heard one series should fail to hear the other, because they constitute between them a unique compendium of everything the budding playwright (and what a loathsome phrase is 'budding playwright') should know and not know. For that matter, no person in his senses would miss any pronouncement made by a man of my standing and education. Please do not forget that I am a member of the P.E.N., the Friends of the Academy of Letters, and WAAMA. In anticipation of an imperative public demand, I am negotiating for the hire of the Theatre Royal in Dublin for my lectures. Watch this newspaper for an important announcement.

My Qualifications

Some people may be inclined to question my qualifications for advising on the don'ts of drama. The fact is that nobody in Ireland knows more about bad plays than myself. Since 1932 I have written 156 of them. Bar sixteen, the whole lot of them have been rejected by the Abbey, and rejected with the arrogant brusquerie of the monopolist. The other sixteen they pretend never to have received, which means that they have lost the manuscripts. Even easy-going people will admit that this is a nice pot of tea. One hundred and fifty plays means 2,400 characters, 650 changes of scene, and heaven knows what other concomitant complexity. When my friends were out enjoying themselves,

I was in a back room engaged on the Homeric tasks of creation. All this labour is thrust aside by the Abbey directors as trash. Trash it may be, but even the trash of the Irish Writers', Artists', Actors' and Musicians' Association is, surely, worthy of better treatment.

The Broad Canvas

Some of the plays, it is true, would set the producer a problem. In one of them, a negro insurrection is crushed with the assistance of 56 frenzied elephants. My real idea had been to provide congenial, artistic employment for some of our girthy intellectuals, but the play was rejected because conceit and the role of an elephant's hind legs do not go together. When WAAMA gets into proper working trim, I intend to get all this reconsidered. Superheated pressure will be brought to bear on the theatre moguls.

In another play there is a desperate storm at sea. Masts, funnels and lascars are carried away by the roaring sou'-easter. The schooner ultimately founders on the stage with all hands, the captain, sea-dog that he was, reading extracts from *Irish Times* leading articles as he is engulfed in his noble death.

The *Panzercorps*, coping-stone, *raison d'être* and *sine qua non* of the strategy devised by the German *Oberste-heeresleitung*, will, according to the *Führer*, achieve *so oder so* a decision in the east.

These are the last, moving words that are heard as the sodden curtain descends on the foaming stage.

Directions for Use

This strange and stimulating play was accompanied, of course, by a memorandum explaining how the difficult storm and sea effects could be got with the assistance of mirrors and wires. Nevertheless, the piece was turned down. No reason was given, but I heard through a friend that it was considered unsuitable for a Dublin audience because the cast did not contain a young girl who has been done wrong, a tyrannical ecclesiastic and an impecunious gentleman with a Dublin accent, who drinks stout and makes uproariously funny remarks every time he opens his mouth.

I will have more to say on this subject in a day or two, and by heavens it will be worth reading.

xii

'Snoring' Owls

Sir, – About three or four years ago two owls took up residence in a barn in my place in the West. They are large birds, grey-white. They make a snoring noise. Every evening at dusk they fly out for the night, returning in the morning. They are unperturbed by the presence of people or noises due to workmen, etc. I noticed recently that there are five owls. They must have had a family. Some say they are Arctic owls. Does any reader know? 'QUERY.'

Letter to *Evening Mail*.

Owls me granny!

It is queer how certain people, when perplexed, rush to the least likely of conclusions. It is a thing I cannot understand at all.

Let 'Query' make a few little investigations on his own. When the 'owls' have retired to rest, let 'Query' steal up to their habitation, slither in without 'waking them, and run a finger up their legs. My bet is that he will encounter the unmistakable undulation of corduroy. His nose will rankle with the stench of oil paint, and his feet may stumble on fearfully interesting books littered about the floor. For the 'owls' are immigrant flyboys.

'I noticed recently that there are five owls.' Yes, and nine or ten. They come and go like little swallows, migrating to Conamara, Achill, and wherenot, looking on the land of Ireland with a listless liquid eye. 'Some say they are Arctic owls.' Change 'Arctic' to 'Arty', and I'm with you.

I had a little conversation with one recently.

He: Have you read Kafka? (*pronounced Kafker.*)

I: Of course. (*slight frown.*)

He: D'you *like* his work? (*how intense are those velvet eyes!*)

I: Not frightfully, actually.

He: I'm not terribly surprised, really. Kafka is too sweet and tenuous for you, I'm sure. He somehow lacks that tough metaphysical quality that is so typically Irish.

xiii

I heard a queer story the other day in the course of personal conversation with an officer of the Air Corps. He said he was on reconnaissance duties at about 2,000 feet above Dublin when he saw in the air some distance from him a strange object closely resembling a well-nourished jack-intellectual attired in tights. The officer's guess was that some ballet people had been practising, and that one of the lads threw an unbelievable leap that brought him into the higher altitudes. He was falling slowly, said my aviator, and seemed to have a course set for Bremen.

All this gave me furiously to think.

I went away muttering '*tour en l'air*' and other little trifles I have learnt from my compendium of ballet jargon. My own hero in the old days, incidentally, was Fokine. Diaghileff I knew and liked, a strange genius of a man if there ever was one. But Fokine was the daddy of them all, and an exemplary family man among a crew of roués. Pavlova I met in Vienna. It was not long till a copy of the first book of O'Growney* found its way into her bag. Thereafter began a philological kameradary that was ended only by the ineluctable dialectic of life. I still have her letters, all written in the worst Irish I have ever read.

*Father Eugene O'Growney's *Simple Lessons in Irish*.

xiv

Pax Hibernica

According to a report of a court case in a recent issue of the *Drogheda Independent*, a gentleman complained that serious damage had been done to his face.

Justice: You say that you had two black eyes, a split lip and nose.
Witness: Yes.
Justice: All in one blow?
Witness: Yes.

It is fairly clear that somebody had a very large fist or somebody else had a very small face.

I am afraid the country is not half settled yet. A recent issue of the *Clare Champion* is devoted mainly to 'Remarkable disclosures . . . gangsters at Ballyvaughan . . . stolen rabbit traps . . . youths charged with breaking into dwellinghouse . . . fisherman drunk and disorderly, assaulting sergeant . . . iron stakes disappear . . . presentation of revolver and assault at Corofin . . . failure to admit Guards . . . larceny of shoes and carrots . . . drunk on the public street . . . charge of maliciously setting fire to three lorries . . . theft of turf.'

And any amount of no lights on bicycles.

XV

Long, Long Ago

Today my peerless drawing-pen turns back a page of history. The picture shows certain long-defunct national personalities belting down the Tim Healy Pass at fifty-six miles an hour with no less than Orby, Troytown, Scarva More and Angel between the non-

existent shafts. In addition to The Big Man*, who is seated quietly inside, the distinguished company includes Thady the Shaughraun, Bould Phelim Brady (the member for Ardmagh, sitting in the nationalist interest), Willie Reilly (M.P. for Cavan), Savourneen Dheelish, the Star Doyle, Tim O'Shenko *père* (astride the Boss Croker's Orby), and the Shader Fotrell.

They have heard that a new and repressive act has been passed and they are on their way to Dublin Castle to drive their vehicle through it.

The Plain People of Ireland: How could they be coming down the Tim Healy Pass? Sure that place didn't exist at all before Willie Cosgrave's time.

Myself: There you go, trying to get me into a political argument. I have nothing more to say today.

*i.e. Charles Stewart Parnell.

41

xvi

The economic *bloc* of my Dublin WAAMA League have now nearly perfected their arrangements for inaugurating the Myles na gCopaleen Central Banking Corporation.

This bank will, of course, practise (and practise right up to the very hilt) the accepted banking game of usury, and will live in some gilded shambles that will be designed by our own little buck-intellectual, ballet-hooligan, verse-mouther and wearer of custard coloured shirtings, to wit, Mr. Claude ffoney. A sum not exceeding £31 10s. 0d. will be charged for current accounts, and admission to the bank's premises will entail a fee of sixpence a time, the management reserving absolutely their absolute right to refuse admission in their absolute discretion and no reasons given. No telephone calls will be dealt with or callers interviewed.

What is Behind the Move?

What, one may well ask, is the necessity for still another bank?

I will explain as simply as I can. The Myles na gCopaleen Central Banking Corporation will not only discount short-term bills drawn on maturing debentures ready and on call, but will also issue credit 'zoning' coupons *pari passu* with movements in and out of the Sterling Equalisation Fund, not, as heretofore, on unliquidated Treasury balances or on the unredeemed 'brokerage' transactions of the holding companies, but also the semi-consolidated note flotations of the *rentiers*. The holding houses will not receive 'discounted' bonds save where the *rentier* cartel has adequate marginal operation to offset any drain of 'dead money' caused by the premature amortisation of trustee-held debentures. That is the whole thing in a nutshell.

Desperate and bitter efforts are being made to dish this revolutionary innovation. The vested interests are pale with fear. The Banks' Standing Committee (from whom all authority is derived) has had to sit down. The Currency Commission has offered me a seat on the board ('two if you can use them, old man') provided I have 'a bit of sense'. Sense I will have if need be, but the cheque will require to be pretty fat.

According to Labour spokesmen, the national credit is at present in the hands of private profit-taking banks, who manipulate it to their own advantage. Where will we be when it is in the hands of my own bank only? What will happen to undiscounted 'suspense' issues, which were hitherto converted into call-money by the holding houses?

In the kingdom of the blind the one-eyed man is banker.

xvii

Information Please

Is this † a dagger which I see before me?
(These are known as 'brackets of parenthesis'.)
These – (gas) – are gas brackets.

† It is.

xviii

I am rather pleased at the reception given to my book, *An Béal Bocht**. It is gratifying to know that an important work of literature receives in this country the recognition that is its due. Scholars, students, men-about-town, clerics, T.D.s, ladies of fashion, and even the better class corner-boys have vied with one another in grabbing the copies as they pour from the giant presses. How long will the strictly limited edition of 50,000 copies last? A week? A month? Who can tell? Suffice it to say that you cannot order your copy too soon. Paper difficulties make it doubtful whether another edition of 50,000 will be possible, in our generation at any rate.

43

That Strange Thing Genius

For a while we were thinking of trying on the London gag of calling the first edition the third, 'first and second editions sold out prior to publication.' We decided against it, fearing that the all-powerful WAAMA would be on our tails for some breach of their high moral code.

About the book itself, it is, indeed, fine stuff. It is the first thing of the kind ever published. You can look out any day now for a deluge of imitations. Refuse all substitutes. Every genuine copy bears the name, 'Myles na gCopaleen'. It is a bitter, yet, a kindly book. It is a chastening and salutory performance. One educated man I know has compared it to Dante's –

The Editor: Our advertising rates may be had gratis on request.

Myself: This is a high-class literary discussion.

The Editor: It is a blatant puff. Everybody has to pay for that kind of thing.

Myself: Of course, if Art means nothing to you, if the lonely and god-like artist, fashioning and creating in solitude, is to be denounced as a commercial hack, a gobdaw on the make –

The Editor: This is more of it.

Myself: Get back to your own page and play with your Panzerdivisionen!

*Published December 1941 (and later translated as *The Poor Mouth*).

xix

Let us suppose you have £16,000 invested in War Loan, a mere £2,000 in Shangcoe Tin Mines, Limited, £3,000 in the Argentine Patent Glue Corporation, not to mention a paltry £5,000 on deposit in a bank in Athlone without the privity of the income tax authorities. With this financial background there is only one thing that prevents you adopting the role of the Irish

Marxist intellectual. I mean the absence of a beard. Here is where I come to the rescue and strike my own little blow in the class war. I can grow a beard on your face in 16 hours, and all for the price of a front stall in the Abbey.

My Patent Beard Food is queer stuff. I do not mind admitting that there is a foul smell from it and that you must keep to your room once you have rubbed it into your jaws. But the following day you will be as bearded as the pard and much more formidable-looking, and the mass of hair will hide from the world the fact that you wear twenty-five bob silk shirts. You are now fully equipped. You can sit in a public house and talk about dialectic materialism as your jewelled fingers toy with a glinting noggin o' Courvoisier.

My Beard Food, of course, can be used by other classes of unpleasant people. Writers, poets and painters, whose work is so bad that they dare not maintain an ordinary appearance, will find the Food invaluable. No matter how often they have tried unsuccessfully to grow a beard the old-fashioned way, they can now take heart. A five-bob bottle will get them farther than a few badly-wanted lessons in drawing.

There is a 5% discount for schools and families.

XX

The brother takes a poor view of the war.

He does?

He says you'll see Spain in before Easter.

How does he know that?

He does be across in London buying paper bags and twine. He says we have no idea. He gives the war another ten years, twelve with Spain in. Himself and Mr Carse had a long talk in a private hotel where the brother stays.

Who is Mr Carse?

An English pal.

Is Mr Carse in the confidence of the British Government?

The brother says he is the first Englishman he ever met that has his head on the right way. A great friend of Ireland, too, married to a Cork girl, so the brother says. Mr Carse takes a very poor view of hostilities beyond in America.

I am sorry to hear it.

Says you'll see a conflagration in South America before Easter. The Latin blood will have to come out somewhere, so Mr Carse told the brother. A world-wide conflagration, the end of which no man can foresee. Them were his words.

It is a bleak look-out.

And then Communism after the war, the dogs in the streets driving around in motor-cars, not a fluke you can call your own and some gobdaw above in Dublin Castle telling YOU AND ME what to do and singin' the Red Flag. Big workin' class flats everywhere you go, and every man of us walkin' round in overalls. Dublingrad, eh?

It is hardly a cheering prospect.

The brother's putting all his money into blankets and fur-coats and valuable articles of cutlery. Real property, he says, is your only man. No fear of him being caught out, or Mr Carse either. Two cute boyos.

Thank you very much for the tip.

Conclusion

The Plain People of Ireland: Have you nothing to say?

Myself: Amn't I saying plenty?

The Plain People of Ireland: But this is Christmas Eve.

Myself: O! I wish to take the opportunity of wishing you all a very happy Christmas and a preposterous New Year.

The Plain People of Ireland (delighted): Thank you very much. A happy and merry Christmas to yourself and to all of the *Irish Times* at Number Thirty-one.

Myself: Thank you. You will send me a card?

The Plain People of Ireland: Of course.

Myself: With snow, robins, holly, black cats, mistletoe, and the old coach-and-four?

The Plain People of Ireland: Of course.

Myself: Thank you, indeed, brothers, and farewell.

2

Education

In which Myles na gCopaleen begins the instruction of his people in earnest, exposing hypocrisy and pretension howsoever manifested. Fallacies concerning the national language are set to rights and certain members of the journalist and author classes castigated. An uncompromising moralist in a disturbed world, Myles has many battles ahead, yet he fearlessly reveals episodes from his own tortured private life, which may serve as object lessons to his followers.

i

News for the Kiddies

Readers will recall my book handling service, which enables non-brows to give visitors the impression that they can read. A special Junior Service is now available for precocious youngsters who loathe piano practice. Their books of scales and arpeggii will be handled for a small consideration, carefully smeared with toffee-stains, plain dirt-stains, blots, chocolate smears, crude drawings of square men, and a thousand other little signs of constant use.

Why not teach your boy to be a cheat and a liar? He will have to match his wits against people of your own kidney when he goes out into the world.

ii

The other day I did something that I am pleased to consider smart. I went into a chemist's shop and said:

'Have you any cigarettes?'

'No,' the lady said in surprise. 'We don't sell cigarettes.'

'Neither do tobacconists,' I snapped, 'so I thought I might as well be told "No" here as anywhere else.'

The lady was ugly enough to have some little wit.

'I could sell you a pound of bath salts,' she said.

'I do not smoke bath salts,' I answered. 'Nor for that matter,' I continued warmly, 'do I empty tins of tobacco into my bath and wallow in the yellow floating mess like some lathered and sea-weed-tangled Neptune.'

'Have you a bad chest?' the lady said.

'It is not too sound,' I admitted. 'The family was always a bit weak in that quarter. The eldest girl is very delicate.'

'Because if you have asthma I could give you a packet of asthma cigarettes.'

I managed to give a wheeze at this stage.

'If you come up here to the quiet end of the shop,' she said, 'I could slip you a packet of twenty.'

The end of this anecdote is in a tenderer key. We went that evening to the pictures. The little hand, soft and pink as a robin's waistcoat, lay quietly in my hairy paw and all about us was the choking stench of incinerated ragwort. Patrons coughed and spluttered and tried to glare back at me through watery fume-bleared eyes. But I gazed happily at the screen, determined to love my Annie in the old high ways of love.

iii

Loquitur

Had a letter yesterday from the married sister. Bags of stuff there, any God's amount of tea and sugar and bacon. Coal, too.

Where?

Above in Belfast.

Then why do they be coming down here by the train-load for feeds?

To get the full of their bags of the hard stuff, man. Scotch rossiners. Can't be had for love nor money above. They don't go in much for stout there at all, nearly all the short stuff. Great men for lifting the little finger, so the married sister says. Down here now every day, droves of them in every street drinking us out of house and home.

Is that the way?

Watch them in any pub, man, throwin' whiskey around like snuff at a wake. I can see ourselves being left short in the near future. I mentioned it to the brother. He views the situation with concern. Takes a poor view of Dublin being sucked dry by the Orangemen. Says smaller things than that have led to trouble in the past. Be Gob, says the brother, I never seen an Orangeman without a mouth on him! Them rallies they do have on the twelfth, they do spend half the time stuck in tents letting the stuff back out of bottles. Then out with them full of fight, all on for skinnin' the nearest Sinn Feiner. The half of them go home with their heads open, of course. They do go for one another at night-time.

A somewhat unruly class.

I see District Justice Goff does be giving out the pay above in Dundalk. There does be scenes there of a Sunday. Lurry-loads of lads down from the north for a day's jarring and then a couple of dozen up for bad language and kickin' the belly off a Guard. O very adjacent. You'd get the ear bitten off you there of a Sunday, so the brother says.

A turbulent and implacable people.

O a nice crowd. Hand me over that hat, I must luv ye and lave you. Thanks. It's not me best hat, as the man said, but it's me only one. Bye-bye!

Good-bye to you.

iv

I wonder is it generally known that a famous worker in the sphere of psychology was accustomed to call his bank balance (jocosely, of course) his 'Freud Potatoes'?

Let me pass from that to another branch of study. Between several universities and one institute a large number of persons are making a living out of monkeying about with what they are pleased to call Old and Middle Irish. The value of their services may be gauged from their ignorant use of these very terms. Old Irish is not, of course, Old Irish at all. It is New Irish, the newest Irish that is known to us. What we speak and write today is Old Irish – namely, that first fresh Irish after it has suffered the ageing changes of fifteen hundred years. Our children will speak an older Irish still. 'Middle Irish' is a meaningless term (actually), because the mid-point of our linguistic time-continuum is perpetually shifting to compensate for the ever-ripening bloom of 'Modern Irish.' I admit that I am thinking in centuries, but who's going to stop me?

Furthermore

Consider this phenomenon in relation to the human body. When we are born we are lucky if we are a foot long, but at least we have the good fortune to have our hips in the middle. Note, however, that our hips remain immovably in the same place, unlike Middle Irish, which is continually moving in pursuit of the head of the ever-lengthening corpus. To put it another way, the human body does not 'grow up,' but grows downwards and upwards from a static centre. There must, therefore, be a tiny central part of us which grows only laterally with the years. This segment of bone and tissue is, therefore, stronger and solider than the rest of the body, because it has not been weakened by horizontal as well as lateral expansion. Hence we have proved that the Irish language is unlike our bodies.

And again

Think, also, that the Irish I write in this newspaper is not only Old Irish (as I claim it to be), but also (given time) Middle Irish and even Early Irish. Time will alter it and custom stale. It will recede to be a part of the world's literary heritage, like Homer and Seoirse Moore.* Always remember that I am writing, not merely passing trash to stuff a small hole in a businessman's day, but also medieval texts to puzzle those who will attend the Institute of Advanced Studies a thousand years hence. Make allowances for the complexity of my task, and be respectful when you are reading what may yet be hailed as one of Ireland's most valuable pre-historic treasures.

Perhaps some kind mathematico-philologist will work out a formula that will explain what I mean more clearly. Some of your men in the Institute should have a shot at it. Tomorrow it may be too late.

ʼi.e. George Moore, the Irish novelist (1852-1933).

V

What time is it by your gold watch and chain? Surely it's not that time! Listen, would you lend me four and sixpence? I drank a glass of weedkiller with me dinner above in Bachelor's Walk and I want to hire a stomach-pump to bring out to the Phoenix Park, I'll find a corner beyond there at the polo ground and see whether I can save me life. Well lend me two and fourpence and I'll buy a pound of butter and stuff it down me neck, paper an' all, BEST IRISH CREAMERY BUTTER, made in glorious Phillipstown under ideal conditions, untouched by hand. I can see you don't believe me. Well, when my poor racked body is being laid to rest, perhaps you will pay me the tribute of a silent tear.

> Gone from sight but not from memory,
> He lies in his lonely grave today,
> One an' all we done our best,
> But we could not make him stay.

Inserted by Gus, Paddy, 'Mims', Uncle Peter and all at Number 84.

The police are anxious to interview a man with whom deceased was seen conversing at the corner of Poolbeg Street on the Tuesday.

vi

Dog bites man. O.K., we know that ain't news, no good newspaper man would try to make a story out of that. But man bites hot-dog, is that news? Man chases cat, is that news? Well-known dog elected to Board of Bank of Ireland, is that news? Puce-faced usurer fights ferret, how about that? If over-zealous Customs men at Dundalk insist on searching the bags under your eyes, is that news? If ebullient zestful Myles na gCopaleen quips in Dublin's swish uptown Shelbourne Hotel that the Americans and Japs are 'Pacifists', is that news? JOCKEY RIDES STRAIGHT RACE AND DOES HIS BEST TO WIN! Would ace-reporter Clark Gable tear out the front page for that and hold everything for a re-plate?

The word 'news' is composed of the initials of north, east, west, and south – news from all quarters, see, STOP THAT!

The Plain People of Ireland: What?

Myself: Biting your nails.

The Plain People of Ireland: Sorry!

vii

I hear that the Clondalkin Paper Mills are fiddling with the idea of pulping limited quantities of the Abbey Theatre audience. Technicians believe that paper made from this pulp, while some-what coarse for half-tone illustration, would stand up to the stress of modern printing machines.

'Naturally we could not let the mills have more than small quantities, at the beginning, at any rate,' a prominent Abbey director told me yesterday. 'You may take it that the whole idea is as yet experimental. We have not taken up the matter with the Department of Supplies. Large-scale or reckless pulping of our audience would only be agreed to in circumstances of extreme emergency. You may take it that we have the situation under constant review.'

Last week by way of experiment fifteen small civil servants were pulped. The result was a coarse grey cardboard which is considered suitable for the manufacture of ersatz bee-hives.

Keats, incidentally, was once almost stung to death by a swarm of bees. His body was completely covered with the tiny red marks of the stings. He laughingly referred to this virus-charged rash as his 'bee-hives'.

Whom We All Know

No lover of humbug is pipe-smoking pullover-wearing Roscommon-born poetry-reading gum-chewing pernicious-anaemia-suffering pig-eyed snub-toed pallour-skinned pug-toothed wall-faced –

The Plain People of Ireland: Come on, hurry! Who?

Myself: Alright, if you can't have patience I won't tell you at all.

viii

I am glad to say that I have been able to do something about the tobacco shortage. I have for immediate disposal 48 bags of second-hand smoke. Some friends have kindly saved up their smoke for me by exaling it into bags I had given them for the purpose. Forty of the bags are Virginia, five Turkish, and the remaining five a special 'Cruiskeen Mixture,' consisting of all sorts of tobacco-smokes and smells and public-house fumes.

You suck the bags as shown in my sketch, and exhale into a spare bag which I supply. When this is full, you return it to me and I make you an allowance on it. Easy, isn't it?

ix

Just as we go to press (what do *you* want? Who? He's not in) just as we go to press I learn that another of my books has been banned. (What? Leave them in the corner there. No, he didn't leave any empties for you) Now this is monstrous. It is monstrous, monstrous, do you hear me, to suppose that I COULD submit to having my writing, my writing, man, choked, stifled, thwarted and stunted by these anonymous smut-glutted muck-butchers who buy my books and send marked copies to the authorities. (Will you please leave that DOWN, I can't have anything in this office without it being pawed and messed about) Where was I? Yes. How can the Irish artist hope to live in such a country? How can he create something which is fine, taut, sensitive in an atmosphere that is fouled by the incessant exertions of thousands of unknown muck-rakers? And submit to the summary confiscation and suppression of great works of art? How can he win out against blank ignorance and prejudice and a corrupt slimy smugness (Here, run out and get me one and tenpence worth, it's near ten) that erupts like the sigh of a submerged rhinoceros in a plague-ridden Malayan swamp? Is it any wonder our artists flee the country in angry despair? (No, I'm not finished yet, I've only a third of the stuff done, shut up and let me work!)

X

And another thing.

Meeting in the Mansion House by the Society for Intellectual Freedom. Please state your point of view. Where do you stand in this matter. Come out into the open. Mr George Bernard Shaw. Thirty shillings received with thanks. Hoping for continuance of your valued patronage and with best thanks. Calendar for 1942 by the Irish Society for Intellectual Freedom. A thought for every day. You can lead an Irishman to water but you can't prevent him drinking porter. Principle of compulsion repugnant to every right-thinking Irishman. I, A.B., do solemnly swear that I will devote my life to the repeal of the Censorship Act. Meetings, lectures, pamphlets, study circle every Wednesday. A prominent novelist will address the meeting. Collection. Write to your T.D. Banning of Kate O'Brien's book. Laughable were it not so tragic. Lady friend. Told me it was the most moving and consoling book she had ever read. Indeed? Well you will be surprised to hear it is banned in Ireland. Wot? Benned in Ahland? Bet wy? Just one tiny reference. Ao. And then in Heaven's name look at Havelock Ellis. Studies in the Psychology of Sex. Treated with great restraint and delicacy. Heartily recommend it, copy should be in every home. Invaluable manual for every right-thinking Irishman. Krafft (durch Freud) Ebbing. Mr Shaw is very annoyed. The great and sublime mysteries of life treated as laughing-matter. Guttersnipes cracking dirty jokes about motherhood in Synge Street in 1869. And of course the cream of the joke is that Halliday Sutherland's book received ecclesiastical approval prior to publication. Now banned. I will not stand for it, do you hear, I will not stand for this bestial censorship. Take my own books. Who but a madman would dare to suggest that they are not works of genius? I tell you I will not have it, I will not have it do you hear me, I will go and live in Paris and then you will all be sorry, another great Irish artist driven into exile.

There is another side to this question. Tiny trash-factors who would never be heard of otherwise have a fine opportunity for making noise when a formal ban is placed on some poisonous little eructation for which they have been responsible. They and Anatole France become brothers under the skin. They become persecuted 'artists' and begin to read the *Observer* in the train on Monday morning. They like to think they are part of the world's great 'writing' family. Theirs is the feeling of a baby at its first pantomime – it wants to go up on the ruddy stige an sy its little piece too ain't it sweet, Rewby. There's just more than far too much of this writing and literary guff-spewing in this country, too many nonentities shouting at us. Burn everything that's been published in the last decade and what have you got? (Got a ruddy fire, George, a ruddy fire! Call that nothing, cocky?)

Thank heavens all my own books are banned. If they weren't, and if people could see for themselves the trash that was in them, would I be invited to any more poetry-readings?

xi

A funny thing happened a few weeks ago. A group of intellectuals were gathered in a back room in Dublin tearing out hair and beard in handfuls over the filthy, iniquitous (I will not stand for it, do you hear) Censorship Act. One jack-beardie flew into fearful tantrums, swore and cursed and cried, and screamed that he would stand this country no longer, and, as he had failed to get an Exit Permit, nothing remained but to commit suicide. A few half-hearted attempts were made to dissuade him, but there was nothing doing. It was time, and high time, somebody did *something*, do you hear me. He wrote out a few theatrical notes of farewell to his loved ones, then shook hands solemnly with his fellow-artists, and left the room. Conversation on literary topics was continued in a somewhat chastened tone, most people present feeling that they had witnessed something that was rather fine.

After a brief interval the would-be suicide reappeared and sat down with fierce ill-humour. 'That damned gas rationing,' was all he would vouchsafe. He has since obtained a post with the Wexford Board of Health and Public Assistance and is stated by his superiors to be diligent and zealous in the discharge of his duties. That's what good long walks in the country does for you.

Tomorrow is St. Patrick's Day. Sir Myles na gCopaleen (the da) will present shamrock to the villagers and tenantry down on his estates. Not to be outdone, certain Dublin newspapers will once again publish leading articles in the Irish language. This done, their duty for the year is discharged. But stay, they may go further this year. They may also print greetings in English but in Gaelic characters.

The price of shamrock should be controlled in urban areas. Last year at threepence a bunch it was 'the dear little shamrock' and no mistake.

xii

Not everything is finite, competent and intelligible. For example, I often rise in the morning, dress swiftly, but with care, and walk through the glass doors to where my breakfast awaits on exquisite gold plate that is hallowed with a patina conferred by numberless ancestral banquetings. But the food is left untouched. Observe the quick nervous movements of my patent leather shoes as they pick a fastidious path through the coarse mane of the carpet, an Axminster job that was picked up for a song in London's Lime street twenty-eight golden years ago. I have now crossed the floor. I am standing beside the gramophone, and with eagle eye I range the deer park. The face is set with a hard contemplative frown, the body as utterly motionless as a statue in the Phoenix Park. The eyes search on as if looking for something in the calm distant trees. Then comes some change. An enigmatic smile steals upon the face. The figure turns slowly towards the gramophone. The polished sound-box, poised deftly between finger and pink thumb, mirrors the pale turquoise nails. In a moment 'Home on the Range' floods out into the still morning. The food cools despairingly on the table, and, in the old-world rose garden outside, old George desists for a moment from his digging to reflect once again that it is a great pity about the master. He waits philosophically for the crash. And it comes in due time. The record is stopped, carefully removed, smashed to atoms and danced on, to the accompaniment of the sort of cries one would hear from a wild beast.

xiii

There was a play at the Abbey recently called 'The Cursing Fields'. I am sorry I missed it because I knew them well. As lads we were forbidden to have anything to do with the family or play with the Fields boys. The reason was that they all used appalling language. Often old Mrs Fields used to come up the lane at dusk and curse in through the hedge at my parents. Sometimes old Fields himself would swear horribly at me through a window when I would be passing by on my way to school. Even the youngest of them, a stripling of ten, had a repertoire of curse-words that would surprise a sea-faring man. One of the older boys emigrated to the States and is now said to be a respectable and valued citizen there. A thing I doubt very much.

xiv

I was in luck the other evening. I went into a house and found the place bristling with all manner of intellectsects. Nobody sits on a chair on these occasions; you find some little nook on the floor, an arm against a stool, possibly a knee drawn up to rest the pensive chin.

On the hearth rug in a nest of hassocks reclined Mr Peter ffoney, hands, hair and eyes in the middle of a disquisition on French literature. A thin, pink-shaded reading-lamp tinted up the little savant against the velvety eye-glinting gloom, through which the soft, foreign waste-pipe voice moved with the pale charm of gangrene.

Listen!
'Ah! Musset*!'
Short pause. The head goes on one side, the awful gull-grey eyes expanding concentrically, a half-smile playing around the corners of the prune-mouth.
'So young! No, no, you must admit the presence there of a

poet! And such sensibility – such a tortured life! You must remember when he went to Venice with that rascally George Sand, poor Musset so happy, and she . . . .'

Ear now sits on shoulder, exquisite mouth a-droop, corrugation of brow, the high-browsy's high sign.

' . . . . She fell ill, Musset called in the doctor, and of course George, splendid, animal, high-spirited, can think of nothing but to make love to the doctor! Poor little Musset is quite broken, drifts back to Paris, loses interest, neglects his dress, becomes a bit of a savage, you know . . . .' Slight quickening of the pace.

'His family won't speak to him, nor he to them. But the old mother . . . .'

Here the head goes on one side again, a pink flush is seen playing on the senile saggy sag-face, duck-web eye-lids pause in langour upon the orbs.

' . . . . the old mother, whimsical, a little domineering, perhaps, ah but what a heart! She commands him to her afternoon tea, makes the poor fellow talk, listens with such incredible sympathy. Afterwards – you know the story – she calls the family together – picture this rigid, worldly gathering of such cultured people! She talks roundly to them, tapping the floor with her stick . . . .'

Here the recitalist, the eyes glazed with whimsy treacle, the upper lip quivering with pastry-cook passion, lets the pipe-voice travel up two and a quarter incredible tones.

'She scolds them: You . . . simply . . . must . . . be . . . kinder . . . to poor Alfrayd. I've talked to him . . . and he . . . has told me . . . everything. Now, you must not pity him, but I know what the poor boy has been through . . . .'

(Aye and more than Alfrayd has been through it.)

'Take him back among you, soothe him, let him be a man again.'

Who would like a naggin of whiskey with no water?

---

*Alfred de Musset (1810-57), playwright, lover and drinker, was known as the 'infant prodigy of French romanticism'.

63

XV

Home Hints

I have just discovered that a slow fire can be lit up in a jiffy with gramophone records. A record is as inflammable as a bucket of petrol, although it is not a satisfactory substitute for petrol when motoring.

I have also found that the works of Walter Pater burn with a steady blue flame and leave a fine grey residue, not unlike cigar ash. A book by Seoirse Moore will smoulder and emit pungent fumes: it will glow brightly if you use a bellows on it, and even burst into dull yellow flames if you mix a little Proust or a little of Miguel Botticelli's memoirs with it (Miguel was the brother): the residue takes the form of coarse clinkers.

If you want a roaring white carefree conflagration and the feathery residue whipped up the old-world Irish chimney, try some of the masterpieces of Gaelic literature. The modern ones, I mean, with all the nice idioms.

xvi

Yes, yes. Open the dictionary. Gnomon, pillar, rod pin or plate of sundial, showing time by its shadow on marked surface. Time and tide will wait for . . . .

There's one in Clongowes where I was reared, made smooth by the very time it tells. *It is later than you know.* I remember a day I stood staring at it for an hour in a priggish pretence of reverie, hoping I was observed by the masters. Most unusual boy, thinking already of life and time. Must lend him some books. The young clean mind, most beautiful thing of all.

And that is long ago. You know the way in films warm nostalgic music suddenly wells up over the dialogue – meaning: Memory! Then flash back.

xvii

I don't care, I know it hurts, but I'm going to keep on with this cliché act. What's wrong with you?
What?
You don't feel well?
Where were you last night?
Where?
O.
And who with?
I see. Who else was there?
I see. I see. Four o'clock. I see. Well you'll get no sympathy from me, take your long pink salmon's face out of my sight. Let me get back to my clichés. There are certain things that certain people just can't say straight. They insist on a hideous round-about locution. It is awful, it makes me pale with anger. Here are a few examples.

English.	*Sub-chat.*
Everybody	The world and his wife
My bicycle	My iron steed
Ladies	The fair sex
The potato	The humble tuber
A letter to the paper	An effusion; a literary effusion
Tobacco	My lady Nicotine
Dance	Trip the light fantastic
Eat and drink	Partake of refreshment
So-and-so	An extraordinary genius
A one-day movement of the population from the city to the seaside	An exodus

The last example is more in the realm of journalese, a substitute for English invented by newspapermen.
What – ?

One and fourpence?
What's the shilling for?
I see. And the fourpence? What do you want fourpence for?
I see. You like to see the beaded bubbles? Here.
All right. Go away.

Letter

Dear Sir – Just a line to let you know how much I enjoy
your column. Your various quips, sallies, etc., are extremely
clever and are much enjoyed by myself and friends. I do
not read Irish but a friend who is an Irish scholar assures
me that I am missing quite a lot. Your poking of fun at various literary personages etc. is most enjoyable, and, if I may
say so, timely. Hoping you will continue the good work,
yours sincerely, H. L.

Now put nutmeg on that and offer it to your dog. How did
he miss calling the lug who is an Irish scholar 'a Gaelic fan'? Your
various quips, sallies, etc. My various quips, sallies, etc.

3

In Extremis

In which Myles na gCopaleen remains faithful to his calling, despite the quotidian pressures and distractions that assail him as he promulgates his mission in a backward and unworthy land. His own personal struggle in the face of the prejudice and ignorance of humanity may briefly be appeased by recourse to alcohol or narcotics, but he is aware that there will be a heavy price to pay. With mind in turmoil, he warns of the perils of multiple identity.

i

Sometimes the sea comes on me stenching me with salt; coarse shark-soured brine oozes in my veins, the sky widens and opens. My three grandfathers were sailors. Tar and dirt and filthy bacon. Sometimes with my nail I think I can feel the scum of sea water caked on my face. She seems to slip – to loop – down despairingly, then rise gorgingly up square under your feet, and all the time the pained creaking of the harness. The crazy cook has the door locked, he is bathing his sore foot in the tea. The monstrous sea is belching and squirming with millions of coloured fish and rubber-hued whales in its dirty belly. Théo Gautier said it all.

> *Existence sublime!*
> *Bercés par nôtre nid,*
> *Nous vivons sur l'abîme*
> *Au sien de l'infini*
> *Des flots rasant la cime*
> *Dans le grand désert bleu*
> *Nous marchons avec Dieu.*

Walk down to the strand and take a look. See how blank and sterile it all is. It is ravished, eaten, sucked by the sea. It is no good at all, nothing will grow there. It is itself a symbol of death. All life is in the sea, the sea is ever animate, but what it touches it makes barren. My three grandfathers took ship for Port Said because they read a lot of lies about the sea in the *Boys' Own*

Magazine. They articled themselves for ten years and walked into the salty unknown with nothing per skull but small pitiful bundles of belongings, a change of shirt, perhaps, and small things like razors, coloured pencils and Conway's Marine Atlas. The same blood that they had is in me. They were the men that made our empire.

That sea trauma often steals upon me late at night, a gigantic muffling visitation full of warm smells and bitter wind. It is the call of drowned blood. My three dead grandfathers seek to communicate by means of out-of-date marine semaphores. Their stomachs are full of sand and they rock gently where they lie. And I scream in the blankets, knowing too well that all this is but a symbol of their love.

My work suffers. My brain (purchased last week by the Royal College of Surgeons) dilates painfully and it is impossible for me to write my newspaper articles. I mean, consider my life. Consider what my life has been, how *intensely* I have always lived. In an attic into which I was locked, mark you, at the age of twelve, I saw into the heart of the world, I illustrated the human comedy. In a cellar I learnt all history. At some nocturnal fête, in a northern city, I met all the women painted by the old artists. In an old alley off Summerhill I was instructed in the classical sciences. In a magnificent dwelling encircled by the whole oriental world, I accomplished my immense undertaking and spent my illustrious exile. I communicated with my own blood. And now, please, no more questions, I beg of you. Think not ill of an old man, he too had his trials and if he was inadequate at least admit he met them bravely. Not necessarily with a smile, for that is British boy-scout stuff. But resolutely, decently, courageously, in a dignified Irish manner.

Occasionally the bell goes off in the middle of a paragraph. I have to throw down my pen at once and go away. Always, of course, I come back and finish what I was doing, but it does not make things easier. I only mention it to show the lengths to which they will go to persecute me. Sometimes I could swear that they make my cocoa with sea water. It may be better, it may mean vitamins, but it brings back all that blue water past. Such is life, I suppose.

ii

Please do not allow me to disturb you at your work – I can come back some other time – but I have a little complaint I would like to whine about. I spend innumerable brain-hours every day trying to remember and record clichés, and sometimes I do get worn out with the hard difficulty of it all. On the night of the 4th of August (and that's not today or yesterday) I was sitting stupefied after spending three hours compiling about ten of them. I idly picked up the evening paper and glanced at a letter dealing with the local elections. This is what I read:

'I hold no brief for any but would like to see men with no axe to grind returned'.

It is at such a moment that life looks blank and hopeless. The greatest cerebral prodigy imaginable pales beside the casually-executed miracles of the unassuming letter-writer. Hold no brief. Axe to grind. It is enough to take away –

Well, take away what?

One's breath.

And how does it give one to think?

Furiously.

Clichés Clichés Clichés

When is it clear that it makes no difference and that it's all the same?

When all is said and done.

The Plain People of Ireland: Clear that what makes no difference?

Myself: I was only talking to myself.

The Plain People of Ireland: Begob you'd better watch that, that's a very bad sign in a young person, you'll be shoutin at people in the street next.

Myself: Thanks.

iii

All this fuss about the scarcity of rashers and the shortage of feeding-stuffs for animals reminds me of a man I used to know years ago in the County Meath. He was a big bullock of a man, beef to the heels, and early in life he showed certain tendencies that were at one with his appearance. Rashers and bread and tea and cabbage and the like he would not touch, but he would not say no to a nice feed of grass or hay. He was a bit ashamed of his queer palate, and many a time I saw him grazing covertly at the back of his cottage in the evenings. He did not get enough nourishment out of this odd diet, and was not flourishing very much physically. One day he happened to taste a piece of oil-cake and thereafter would hear of no other food. He began to live on oil-cake and gradually grew more and more to resemble a well-furnished prime-conditioned Mullingar bullock. The climax came when he drove three of his own bullocks to the fair and managed to pass himself off as a fourth before a short-sighted Manchester buyer. He got paid for four and was then driven off to the North Wall with the others. Once on board the boat, his game was to wait until she was at sea and then make his way up to the bar and put in the night playing poker and drinking whiskey with the other cattle men. At Liverpool he would have the father and the mother of a breakfast and go home on the next boat. Thereafter he was to be seen at every fair in the midlands. He would buy three bullocks one minute and sell four the next and then off with him again to the North Wall lairages. What became of him at the latter end I do not know. Some people say he got drunk one night when he was below with the cattle waiting for the boat to pull out and that his senses did not return until it was too late. Who knows, Lord Castlerosse may have had a bit of him for breakfast at Claridge's one fine morning long ago. In his own way he was a decent man and spoke Irish at a time when it was neither profitable nor popular.

iv

Excuse me. I beg your pardon. Excuse me for butting in when you're with your friends but could I see you alone for a moment?

If you wouldn't mind coming out for a second, down here to the quiet part of the shop.

Just for two seconds.

Yes, a little private matter, a little personal thing I want to mention to you.

Just come down here where it's private for a moment.

Just a little further bit down, where we can have a word or two alone. Eh?

No, just here, this'll be all right.

Yes, we're all right here. Nothing new with you I suppose? Eh?

Yerrah not at all, lad, sure I'm in a hurry myself. Yes.

Listen, could you lend me a fiver?

Yes, I know. I know. I know. Of course. The rates? Yes. I know. Of course you'd have it back on Thursday next at half past three or if you like I could post it and you'd have it first thing Friday morning.

I know. Yes. I understand. I know.

But it's only a matter of three or four days, I don't want to spend it or touch it, I just want to show a certain party that I have it. Matter of fact the whole thing is a formality, a sort of joke really. Eh?

Yes. I know. I suppose so. Yes.

But I mean it's not as if it was a question of *lending* money or anything like that, it's only for a day or two, just a sort of a formality. I mean, you needn't have the slightest doubt . . . . Eh?

No, I suppose not. Indeed very few of us have it and that's a fact. There's certainly no doubt about that. Yes. Ah yes. Funny thing, I'm always helping the lads out myself, fellow stuck for an odd quid for his digs and so on. Don't always get it back, either.

And now begob I have to laugh, find myself a few bob short. Come on Bill, be a pal. A fiver for three days, what's that between pals? Sure many's the good times we've had together and will again. I could see you right here on Thursday if that suits you better. Now that I come to think of it, I'll be passing this way on Thursday. If you're not here I could leave it for you with Joe. In a sealed envelope, of course. What? I know, but what the hell difference would three days make? I'm stuck, Bill. You're the only man I'd ask and that's the God's truth. I'd have my tongue out by the roots before I'd ask any of that crowd. Eh? Who? *Him*? Oh no thanks. Pardon?

Well I'll tell you what. I think I know where I'd get the other half of it. Could you rally round with two ten?

I know. Yes. O that's true, I suppose.

Listen, Bill, I wouldn't make this confession to anybody else but I'm in a bad jam. I must have a few quid to carry me till Thursday till a certain ship comes home. I know it's tough to ask you for a fiver. Make it a quid and I'll find the rest somehow.

Eh? Yes. I know. I know. Yes.

Five bob! You're not serious. Eh?

I see. Yes. I know, I know.

Well listen Bill, it's not much use but I know you mean well, your heart's in the right place, I won't hurt your feelings by refusing it. Thanks, old man. Nothing strange with you at all, I suppose?

V

Nothing I like better of a damp winter's evening than to go down into the cellar with a few elderly civil servants and by guttering candle-light play poker with four jokers on the belly of a smouldering bag of lime, cracking the while an errant cockroach between my gold-filled teeth. Then up again at midnight for a damn good feed of whiskey and whiting.

The Plain People of Ireland: Well dear knows that's a quare meal – not that you wouldn't need the whiskey after being down below in a dark cellar.

Myself: Sometimes I have rhubarb and lemonade and other times bananas and cocoa.

The Plain People of Ireland: Of course the bananas would be barred now, hasn't been a banana in the country for four years.

Myself: You're right there begob.

vi

I dreamt last night that a fellow said to me, talking of Russia: Did ye know that Guinness's own a lot of property out there? Did ye not know that? Oh, sure, gob, that's well known – they own nearly all Siberia – sure how could they keep themselves goin in hops and so on above in James's Street? Begob the stuff they use there didn't come from England, or from Holland neither. Sure didn't one of the Guinnesses go over there to Russia in nineteen o seven, the year of the Exhibition, and buy up twenty million acres of hops and barley and wrote out contracts for as much more and what's more paid cash on the nail in Bank of England fivers. Sure what are you talking about man. O certaintly. Guinness's was the best customer they ever had over there and damn well they know it. And do you know what I'm going to tell you, they'd do annythin for Guinness's, annything. The Russian is a gas man, but he's a decent man, d'ye see, a hell of a decent man. O certaintly, sure that's well known. Annybody'll tell you that, man.

vii

How vain, how parrot-like the catchword that knowledge is no burden! Sometimes, when wearied with intensive study, I emerge into the fashionable world for a brief hour and bandy words all too meaningless with some nonentity, I am asked to accept this most lying of platitudes in the name of 'conversation'. At such a time one screams. Pity for the human race is quenched, albeit for a brief moment. A strident anger rears itself with menace on the seat of reason. Learning no burden! And to think that I, I, I, who . . . . .

But enough.

I have exhausted all the sources of human knowledge, come finally to the end of all cosmic science; I am master of the learning of every nation, of all tongues dead or living, of every literature, western or in the east. Art in all its uncountable manifestations, every fine externalisation of human sensitivity and loftiness, every work where charm and nobility mix, these things are now commonplace, for me they have the quality of bread. I have lived in all orders of society, have viewed every flux of nature and human artifice, have studied man under every *phasis* of civilisation. I have studied him in the wilderness and wherever he may assemble communally. The influence of creeds, laws, manners, customs, traditions, all, all have been subjected to my personal scrutiny, weighed, considered, often found wanting . . . .

But what an advantage to be able to bring to the study of this vast aggregate of knowledge a penetrative intellect, matured by long meditation and assisted by that absolute freedom from prejudice which permits me to fathom as it were intuitively the profundities of questions apparently incomprehensible . . . . .
But today I cannot write; something gnaws at my vitals, I know not what. And knowledge, forsooth, is no burden . . !

To a man in my position there might yet seem one unfailing source of felicity and joy. One might think that I could have discovered the perpetual spring of happiness in the sensibility of the heart. Alas, no! To me this is a sealed fountain. Here then is a thing that is outside my perception. Perhaps in my so complex organisation there is a peculiarity – say a deficiency, if you will. The fact is that I am a man without affections. That is not to say that I have no heart, for I am susceptible of deep emotions. But never, do you hear me, never for individuals. I am capable of rebuilding a town that has been razed by cruel war; of restoring a colony that has been reduced by some dreadful visitation of nature; of carrying out large-scale drainage works where swollen waterways make miserable the lot of peasants; of admitting to the human community races and peoples not hitherto welcomed by reason of epidermic pigmentation; of visiting with grandiose derision political knaves who would levy unjust taxes; of redeeming to liberty a horde of verminous captives. These things I would do. But, mark you, *in deadly secret.* For in truth, void as I am of all self-love, public approbation is . . . . . nothing to me. It is hollow, shameful, a fake. It is to me . . . . useless. I do not want it. Offered, I refuse it. The individual never touches my heart. And woman! Woman is to me . . . . a toy. What are all women? Playthings for a brief hour. And man? Man is a machine. To the human colony on this earth I can give nothing but my pity. Pity is all it can expect from me.

viii

What is the nature of clockwork?
It is regular.
And what is the nature of daylight?
It is broad.
What usually is an exaggeration?
It is gross.
What nourishing confection is associated with order?
Apple-pie.
Quoties dat qui cito dat?
Bis.*
Quid?
Quid. Quoque 10/-. What condition of external recreation is this cliché act?
Played out. Must think of something else.

*Bis dat qui cito dat: Twice gives he who quickly gives.

ix

I was reading this newspaper the other day (really, I must get a grip of myself, I simply must stop this morbid habit) well annyway as I was sayin', I was perusing this valuable publication the other day when I came across this:

'Just imagine, 25,787 families, fathers and mothers, sisters and brothers, eating and sleeping, having babies and dying in one room.'

It was the year of the split, I think, when I last visited that vast apartment. Ranging away (as far as the eye could see) was that limitless panorama of humanity, every one of 25,787 families, 79,421 persons in all. On the day I called they were occupied as follows:

Eating	28,690
Sleeping	32,711
Having babies	14,832
Dying	3,188

Of course, when I was there, the number in the room had risen from 79,421 to 79,422, an increase of .000000000213 per cent (circulating). And that one intrusive unit was eating.

Yes. O indeed faith well I remember.

X

I called into a house the other night to see some friends. I found them crouched over a very evil-smelling fire. A solitary candle was the only light. We were talking there for a while when I noticed with a horrible start that there was an extra person in the room, a tall thin young man who was sitting in the background trying to read a volume of Proust. It was not the oddity of his detachment from the rest of the group which surprised me so much as his appearance. His appearance was gruesome in the extreme. His forehead and the front of his head had been hacked away as with a crude knife.

'Who is your man?' I whispered.

'O him? That's the cousin. Smartest man in Ireland, doing great work at Trinity.'

'But – '

'O that? He has brains to burn. We couldn't get any turf yesterday, so we asked him would he help us out. Most obliging chap, always reading books.'

'You don't mean to say -'

Nature Note

All over my garden I have tiny wooden houses stuck on poles. I call them tantrums because the birds fly into them.

xi

Puff, puff, puff.

Under the connecting feeling of tropical heat and vertical sunlights, I brought together all creatures, birds, beasts, reptiles, all trees and plants, usages and appearances, that are found in all tropical regions and assembled them together in China or Indostan. From kindred feelings, I soon brought Egypt and all her gods under the same law. I was stared at, hooted at, grinned at, chattered at, by monkeys, by parroquets, by cockatoos. I ran into pagodas; and was fixed, for centuries, at the summit, or in secret rooms; I was the idol; I was the priest; I was worshipped; I was sacrificed. I fled from the wrath of Brama through the forests of Asia; Vishnu hated me; Seeva laid wait for me. I came suddenly upon Isis and Osiris; I had done a deed, they said, which the ibis and the crocodile trembled at. I was buried, for a thousand years, in stone coffins, with mummies and sphinxes, in narrow chambers at the heart of eternal pyramids. I was kissed, with cancerous kisses, by crocodiles; and laid, confounded with all unutterable slimy things, amongst reeds and Nilotic mud.

It was the year of the split, I think, when I took to the pipe; one day since then without opium I have not lived. Could not, would not, live. Sometimes I seem to climb up and disappear amid the grotesque scenery of my own dreams; sometimes I emerge fron the fumed sleep, my own nightmare incarnate.

My medical adviser (a slave to the inferior yet cognate preoccupation of laudanum) tells me that I must quit this pipe or perish. Yet my pouch today (a Kapp and Peterson job of 1918) is as well-lined as ever. My immovable leather cheeks have achieved the pattern of a comic leer. Majestic ulcerations pit my mouth. And only yesterday I gave a furtive fill to a certain high-up civil servant who has smoked away the increments of twenty golden years. He need not worry; his name and his shame are safe with me.

Believe this much. If today I was not in this mood of kingly tragedy, expressed in the great stately prose I can write so well, I would make some poor joke about the facility of descent to Avernus, and then the revocare – hic labor, hoc opium . . . . .

And if I did itself, damn the bit of it would you understand, dear reader, Synge Street and all as you went to.

Come round the corner here for a minute out of the breeze till I light me pipe.

Quite suddenly a small dog has appeared in my mind. He is clearly the property of some deceased mandarin. His coat is clipped in the manner of the east; his waist is clipped nearly naked, fantastic pantaloons of hair are made to clothe his legs. He runs rapidly around my head, searching vainly for mice. Suddenly he has grown old. Pathetic white moustaches girdle his old jaws. He lies down.

The walls of my memory have been decorated free of charge by Mr Jack Yeats. Every night without fail there is a display of fireworks –

The Plain People of Ireland: Where?

Myself: Inside in me head.

The Plain People of Ireland: Faith there's one thing wrong with you, it's maggoty drunk you are and nothing else.

Myself: I am tangled in pale grey dreams . . . . vapours . . . .
in my bare feet I stand on the scaly backs of pregnant crocodiles
. . . . pythons curl like mufflers around my neck . . . . my hand
holds the hair of a beautiful dusky slave . . . .

The Plain People of Ireland: Aisy now, aisy there! Did you not
see be the papers where there's goin' to be an end once and for
all to that class of rascality . . . . and licentious . . . . contumelious
. . . . derogatory . . . . dirty sinful foreign literature. Will you
whist man, before you shame us all.

Myself: Eggs of the phoenix . . . . ivory gobangboards . . . .
silver cephalopods fingered by maidens . . . .

The Plain People of Ireland: Yerrah, leave him be, himself and
his pipe and his dirty books.

xii

The other night I awoke to find myself, so to speak, wide awake
in the (pitch) darkness. (All this is a strictly personal matter.)
Matches. The hand goes out. A light splutters. The time? It is
precisely 4.15 a.m. I hold the gold 18-jewel job to my ear. I
recognise the strong urgent beat of the Suisse thoroughbred.
What's this? He has lit a candle. I have lit a candle, rather. For
what purpose? The better to light a cigarette. Cigarette glows
and then the coughing starts. But what's this? A great flaming
torch beside my bed. The candle is worn down to the wad of
paper that is wrapped round its butt. Fed by luscious wax, the
paper blazes enormously. Grotesque luminances play on the
hollow print-crazed face. And what is this that has now
appeared on that 'countenance'? Fear? Yes, FEAR. Fear of fire.
Freud. Small burn in early childhood. Soon the house will be a
mass of flames, the bed spluttering and sizzling as the feathers go
up in smoke. CRASH! The flat hand has descended with a terrible smack, extinguishing the flame amid pungent taper-smells.
Now darkness again, nothing but the ghostly cigarette-glow.
More coughing.

What am I doing now? The half-smoked cigarette has been savagely stubbed down on the expensive bedside table. I am out of bed. The wardrobe. A chair is hastily dragged over to it. Up on the chair. The hands grope into the top, cobwebs and dust and dirt. An old newspaper rattles. 'Connaught Tribune.' Tuesday, 15th of August, 1939. Grope grope grope. I have it. An old dirty violin-case is lifted down. Out it comes in the darkness, a handsome red instrument of great age. I am screwing the bow. The strings are softly touched for pitch, the steel E string tightened with the tiny screw, the others with the pegs. Soon a dreadful wail pierces the night, Tosselli's Seranata. Ah-da-da, da-Da-da-da.

Outside in the front, footsteps are heard. A homing drunk. Tap tap tap. Then the footsteps stop. He is listening. What is this? He has broken into a run. Scared. Unearthly music late at night. Leprechauns' tiny orchestra. Ghosts. Headless violinists, phantom instruments propped against imaginary jaws.

The music has ceased. Bow and fiddle are frenziedly bundled into the case. Up on the chair. Everything is now as before.

Do I go back to bed? No. Hunger. Hollow feeling in stomach. Bare feet patter down cheap linoleum of stairs. Is there anything in the house? Matches splutter, head stuck in cupboard. A lump of bread. No butter. No butter of any kind. Nothing. But what's this? Van Houten, a tin of cocoa. Untouched for six years. A little sugar in the bottom of the bag. Then frenzied action. Cocoa and sugar are recklessly spilled over the bread. Mouth crammed with crunching mess.

Back to bed shivering. Will I straighten out stubbed fag-end and smoke it? No. More coughing. Then sighing. A sneeze. Sleep.

I awake in the cold morning feeling disturbed. I look at the wardrobe, then look away. Rise, wash, dress. Just as leaving bedroom, casually bring chair to wardrobe, mount it, have a look. No violin. Nothing but a dust-caked coat-hanger.

Go downstairs. Take furtive look at kitchen table. Yes. Traces of sugar. Fine cocoa-dust. Crumbs.

And what's this? That dreadful hammering in my head again. I look coldly at my 'breakfast'. I do not touch it. Coat and hat are donned. Out. Going into my office? No. Up to the Phoenix Park to lie all day in the long wet grass.

⋮
xiii

Here is a question which I address preferably to bibliophiles, but bibliophobes are permitted to consider it.

Is it possible to buy a valuable book for a few pence down the Dublin quays? Has it ever been done?

In fact I did put it viva voce to a few people. The answer was always the same.

'Yes, it can and it has. Most of the booksellers know the value of their wares up to a point, but if you are diligent and lucky, you *will* catch them napping. I remember once becoming the proud owner of a first edition of *Childe Harold* for the sum of fourpence. That was in 1928.'

This is all ignorant tosh, of course. In fact it is not possible to buy a valuable book for a few pence and it has never been done, in Dublin or elsewhere, since the world began. I admit, of course, that it is possible to *pick up* a valuable book for a few pence.

'O, that? I picked that up down the quays for a few pence. There's only one other copy in existence and that's in the Vatican library.'

xiv

I know I'm getting too old to run – what the doctor said about my heart the last time he listened to it is not worth repeating – but the other day (nothing if not reckless) I ran into a friend who married recently.

'When are you going to come and see us?' he queried.

'Well,' I said, temporising as usual, 'I'm tied up all this week but I expect to be free next week and I'll give you a ring.'

Then I (made) (my way) home and sat down to my (frugal)

evening meal of hake and cider. When I was finished feeding, I lit a cigarette and started to scan the evening paper. The scansion was all wrong, I couldn't find a decent hexameter in the whole issue. In the middle of my reading I felt the familiar tap on my shoulder. That damned keeper again. I rose with a sigh and followed him into the next room. He opened the great brass-bound chest and took out the ropes, manacles and strait jacket. In a (jiffy) he had me tied up and stuffed me into an old meat safe in the backyard where (perforce) I had to spend the night.

The funny thing is that that friend of mine did not seem to believe me when I said I was tied up all the week.

And why this brutal treatment, you ask. And well you may ask. I am as sane as you are, even as sane as that adjacent and anonymous party, the next. They tied me up because I chose to follow a very old axiom of commerce. I appeared in the street one day with an enormous tray of hot cakes. (Nothing would do me) (only) believe that I would make my fortune in five minutes, that people would be killed in the rush to buy. And I only got put away for my pains, that's what. (Do you get the subtle pun there – *pains?*)

Yes. Sometimes, looking unutterably spiritual in that dated biretta, my considering cap, I look at myself for what I am (and not for what *you* are). Is it not true that I have in this world at least failed to make that personal symbol of (unspeakable) illiteracy, my mark? With Fame I have in fact only that paralytic (if Homeric) butty, a nodding acquaintance. The fact is, there is nothing to me. There are some who hint in that extraordinary un-lit manner, darkly, that I am not even Myles, that I am obtaining money under those quare contradictory men, false pretences (and who ever heard of true pretences?), that I am constantly engaged in the agricultural yet musical occupation of milking this paper to the tune of thousands a year. Who am I then? Mrs Beeton? You see you're talking nonsense. I don't even know Mrs Beeton. And I wish all this would stop, it's (preying) on my mind, it has the heart wore out (of me) with worry. My resignation? Yes, but I have no stamp. How then could I *send* in my resignation? True, I tried to get (in) to talk to the Editor, a man renowned for his expressions, linguistic and facial. It was not, believe me, that I wanted to have a heart-to-heart talk with him – the only heart I ever had was put across me years ago, had the thing in my mouth for half an hour down in Ballylickey during the Tan war. But no your man is not to be disturbed I was told. And why, pray, why, why? Am I that arithmetical symbol of no value in itself but multiplying the number it is placed after, and dividing the decimal number it is placed before, by ten – a mere cipher? No no no, it's not that, but the great man is at work, every muscle in the shapely countenance is being brought into that quotidian drama – he is composing his features.

All I really wanted, of course, was the loan of a quid, pay it back for CERTAIN on Thursday next at 3.30. A quid may not seem much to you, but what explosive respiratory paroxysm of the nostrils is not to be performed at a quid nowadays?

XV

See, I'm at the window now. I pull aside the corner of the blind and peer out. Dismal rain. A sodden figure is making his way through the murk. He is approaching the house, he is going to call. Who can it be? I can scarcely make out his face but there is something familiar about the stride. The clothes too I have seen before. Now I see him! I know who it is. It is myself! I rush down and open the door just as the ring comes. Immediately I am confronted with the question.

'What were you doing at the window?'

'I was looking out for myself,' I nimbly reply.

xvi

I don't know whether this anecdote is in that favourable savouring, good taste, but I'll chance it. I met a friend who is a psychiatrist the other day. As I was talking to him a mutual acquaintance passed. The psychiatrist nodded after him.

'A patient of mine, poor fellow,' he said. 'He's inverted.'

I looked after the poor fellow. Sure enough he was walking on his hands.

That was only by way of that obscure instrument that performs what seems to be an absolutely unnecessary task – a pipe-opener. Today I am occupied with a well-known alternative culinary operation, I have other fish to fry. I want to tell you about how I am going to make a lot of money in 1943. (Dear me, nineteen forty three. How odd that looks. The years, like great black oxen, tread the world, and I am broken by their passing feet. If we go on at this rate we'll all be dead very soon. And the deplorable fact is that we will go on at this rate.)

One makes money by (catering for) some urgent public taste. For example, ladies' stockings. Ladies like wearing stockings, probably because their legs are unsightly. You make the stockings, the ladies buy them, and you become wealthy. But there are already too many people making stockings. One must find some want that is not yet supplied.

My own conviction (I got a week from Reddin* in '35) is that drinking men are not yet completely catered for. I don't mean the four bottles of stout and a half one for the road people. I mean the hard goers. The ones who would drink whiskey out of a horse-trough. I don't think they're looked after properly. They are inconvenienced and interfered with in their gigantic potations by the horde of modest bibblers who infest and disgrace our public houses. And some of them (I say it with shame) women. Port-sharks. A small gin and lime, plee-ezz. Taking up room and interfering with the stern masculine task of large-scale drunkery.

Well I intend to make a stack by opening an exclusive pub. Only men who are in earnest about drinking will be admitted. In appearance the place will be ordinary enough. Nice mahogany counter, quiet snugs, shelves, mirrors, cigarette ads, sawdust, any amount of bottles. But not beer bottles. Whiskey only. And in one respect my place will be absolutely unique. In (the whole place) there won't be a single glass, cup or mug. The whiskey will be served in dainty jewelled horse-troughs. The troughs will be surrounded with kneeling pads of exquisite velvet, and a golden fountain of whiskey will play into the trough to keep the level from sinking.

But stay. I think there is an even simpler way of making money. Yes, I'm getting excited, I think I've had that odd cerebral undulation, a b.w. I think I've hit upon something, I can nearly feel the bruise. Tell me what's wrong with this.

I get a horse and cart. I go from door to door collecting, not waste-paper, but old rope. And the older the better. There must be thousands of tons of the stuff lying around the country, particularly in places like Dun Laoghaire and Cobh. And whereas waste-paper, ladies' stockings, gold or D'Alton's History of Ireland may through some economic freak become unsaleable, everybody knows that you can always get money for old rope.

Do you mind the cuteness of me?

˙Kenneth S. Reddin (1895-1967), District Justice, writer and patriot.

xvii

Do you ever go to the plays? Not the pictures now. The plays. The high-class stuff.

I do an odd time.

The brother went last summer with Mr Carse. Took a very poor view.

Indeed?

Went to d'Abbey Theatre. Never saw such a collection of people in his puff. Some of them in rags and other lads walking around in claw-hammer coats. No smoking allowed. What do you think of that? No smoking. Light up and you're asked to leave. The brother was very amused.

I see.

There was some class of a play going on about a fortune. There's a hat of money there and then where this fellow comes back from America and where d'other lad is for hangin' on to the dough and then there's some row about a girl – O right mad stuff, you wouldn't know which end is the sleeves. And then where d'ould fellow that nobody minded was the winner in the wind-up, thanks very much, delighted with himself and all for marryin' the young one. A little bit near the bone some of the stuff was, so the brother said. A very strict man on that class of thing, the brother.

I understand.

Of course half of the lads that do be at that place do be writin' dirty books in their spare time. All classes of smut, so the brother says. Saints and scholars how-are-ye!

How are you, indeed.

But what took Mr Carse to the fair was the bar. What do you think they sell in the bar? Tell me that and tell me no more.

Intoxicants, I presume.

Not at all, man, coffee. COFFEE. Well look. You could brush Mr Carse offa your sleeve like a flea, so the brother says. A great man for his jar, Mr Carse. Always was. Of course, the brother will take his bottle of stout.

Stout is a nourishing beverage.

Take his bottle of stout with any man. He'll go up as far as four. Thus far and no further. Use it right, the brother says, and it won't hurt you. But Mr Carse's face when he was told coffee was worth all the parsley in the county Cork. The brother was very amused.

4

Quaquaversal Luminary

In which Myles na gCopaleen valiantly perseveres in his tutelage of mankind, though he is increasingly beset by the affliction of multiple identity. Manifold scholarly disciplines are treated, among them the arts of music and theatre, history (embracing railway history), jurisprudence, science (domestic and natural), languages and nomenclature, the marketing and use of whiskey (with a cure for the same) and, as ever, the forging of the uncreated conscience of the Irish race. A man of such consequence will not lack adversaries, however, and now that the seed has been sown, the time for Myles to withdraw from his pastorship may be approaching.

i

I am alone. Before me on a green plate is a solitary apricot, its hue more delicate than maiden's cheek. A silver fruit-knife, exquisitely embellished, rests on the table. I lift the plate carefully and with a (deft) flick of the wrist I have thrown the apricot into the fire. Waste, you say? Perhaps. But think that I have travelled one more step on the road to the complete conquest of the body and its grosser appetites. Is that not worth something? Does the mortification of the flesh no longer mean anything in this strange old world?

But what is this? There is a deafening report! The apricot has exploded (wreaking) what else but (untold damage). My Lew E. Kahn's chairs are blown to bits. Mercifully, however, I am unscathed. (I met a very queer-looking man down in Carlow the year of the split – he was scathed, that's why he looked so odd.) An anonymous apricot by post in the centre of which is concealed an ingenious bomb. My enemies. An attempt on my life, clearly. Just because I choose to speak out fearlessly on vital public issues, some ruffian does not (scruple) to make an attempt on my life. Some wretched Marxist scoundrel or a Phibsborough Trotskyite.

An attempt on my life? If this means that somebody thinks I should die, I hope somebody else will think it worth while to make an attempt on my death. Because this would surely mean an attempt to prolong my alleged life indefinitely and beset it with luxury beyond the dreams of Avar Rice, that notoriously covetous person. Myrtle, myrrh, oysters, goblets of red gold, a

93

carpet of bear's fur, fine ladies, exquisite French hats, rough fellows with whom to dice . . . .

ii

I read the following important notice in a certain family neicepiper.

'Readers who find it difficult to secure the "Irish Times" are requested to communicate with the manager.'

I suppose you've had it happen to yourself. You leave the damn thing on the table and grab a bite of cold viscous pseudo-egg. (Next thing is) the 'Irish Times', inverted commas and all, taxiing down the tar, Mac, taking off, up in the air and then – altitude 5000 feet – stuck up on the ceiling dead flat like a David Allen* job. Reason for this, of course, is the abnormal volume (that perverted book) of hot air in your man's —> leading articles. And mind you, the windows are closed, not a breath of wind out. After a few days the ceiling has so many Hibernian *tempi* on it you might say it's in the jigs. Well, what we want to do is to communicate (don't for heaven's sake write, telephone, call to see him or send a carrier pigeon) with the Manager. He, poor devil, is having the same trouble and wants to know if you see what he sees.

That hammering – that *dreadful* hammering – in my head again.

A Thought for 2d

Rome was not built in A.D.

*A Dublin poster advertising firm.

iii

We Irish people actually are simple, unspoiled God-fearing sophisticated mid-Europeans, cherishing urbanity like a jewel.

It is time that was said, for with us modesty can nearly be a vice. We are extremely nice people. A humble community of persons drawn together in our daily round of uncomplicated agricultural tasks by the strongest traditional ties, closely woven on a diminutive leprechaun's loom, five and six a go and no coupons required. Our conversation – gay, warm and essentially clean – is confined to the charming harmless occurrences of every-day life (and *not*, of course, every-night life, that undesirable Parisian phenomenon). The wild and morbid degeneracy of the outer world does not concern us (save, if you like, to provide mute evidence of the distinction between the Irish race and all others). Our licensing laws are models of their kind. A wise and benevolent administration protects us from backin' alien horses, I beg your pardon, bacchanalian courses. The hateful and dishonest stockmarket manipulations of the great international grain cartels is to us that mysterious ornament, a closed book. What is called 'news' (by which one means the perverted sensationalism of the yellow press) does not concern us. We are not amused. Rumour (that recumbent jewel or lying jade) once had it that a war was going to break out. Nothing ever came of it, of course.

My point is that we are reticent to one another to the point of being taciturn. Our Irish habit of tasteful restraint is carried sometimes a little bit too far. Hence I was pleased when recently a public man was permitted to announce publicly at last that we are, in fact, the best people in the world and consequently better than any other people. But there is another concomitant or epiphenomenal fact that I do wish he had touched upon. I refer to the Irish language. Our native language is the best language in the world and better than any other language ever spoken by that wayward biped, man. The Italian, as you know, is pleasant but without sinews, as too stilly fleeting water; the French delicate but over-nice, as a woman scarce daring to open her lips for fear of marring her countenance; the Spanish majestical but fulsome, running too much on the o; the Dutch manly but very harsh, as one ready at every word to pick a quarrel.

Now we in borrowing from them take the strength of conso-
nants from the Italian, the full sound of words from the French,
the variety of terminations from the Spanish, and the mollifying
of rough vowels from the Dutch: and so, like bees, gather the
honey of their good properties and leave the dregs to themselves. And thus when substantialness combineth with
delightfulness, fullness with fineness, seemliness with portliness,
how can the language which consisteth of all these sound other
than most full of sweetness?

And Irish butter. Where in the whole wide world will you
find anything to compare with it for delicacy of taste, pigment
and texture? In what utopian sty will you find the superior of
the Irish pig? In what gilded haunt of gastro-gnomes in Paris or
distant Trieste will you be given a back-rasher the like of which
you will receive in humblest Limerick bistro? Don't be talking
to me, man.

And comic newspaper writers.

I am certainly guilty of absolutely no exaggeration when I say
that we have one or two 'columnists' in this lovely old cow-
inhabited country that are excelled nowhere as comics. I read
them all every day. They amuse me. Cigarette-racked cackle
though it be, they always give me a good laugh.

iv

I was in the National Museum the other day and came across a
pikestaff, very likely a relic of '98. And do you know, anything
plainer than that pikestaff I have never seen. I was also shown a
small object said to date from early Danish times – a door-nail
from a small palace built in Werburgh Street by Sitric the Silken.
Among all things inanimate and defunct, nothing could be quite
deader than that door-nail. An attendant I met on the way out
(on that manual alternative, the other hand) was as large as life.
He presented a nice contrast to the door-nail, which was as small

as death. I think I heard the attendant refer to me covertly as 'that hatter'. And small wonder.

V

Sir Myles na gCopaleen (the da) has directed the servants employed at the Research Bureau to start work with a view to producing 'the opposite of drink'. This queer phrase was at first taken to mean cubes of solid edible matter which, however, was not food. Several obscure experiments were made on this basis before it was discovered that the grand old man had been studying the pernicious effects of alcohol on the nation's health and was anxious to produce the opposite of this liquid, thinking that its effects would be bound to be proportionately beneficial. Now the Institute has perfected a beverage which is expected to revolutionise human society. It is a pink liquid and after a glass of it you feel rather seedy. A second glass and you are depressed. A third and an appalling pathological morbidity has descended on you. A fourth and you are vainly seeking the loan of a razor from the barman so that you can quietly open your throat in the back snug. A fifth and you are in a condition that does not bear description.

But assuming you get home to bed, what a difference the next morning! The whole house resounds with your thunderous operatic arias, windows are thrown up, backs slapped and your joy at being alive roars in great gusts through the lives of the whole startled community. People stop to watch you in the street in envy and astonishment. The curious effect the liquid has the next morning is called a hangunder.

vi

If you don't mind we'll start off this morning with a little bit of Bach. Some of us are so musical we eat tripe with tuning forks. Ready?

'You shall be wakened. YOU SHALL BE WAKENED. You sha-hah-hah-all be wakened. Wakened. Wakened. You sha-hah-hah-hah-hah-hah-all be way-hay-hakened. You-hoo-hoo sha-hah-all be wakened. Be wakened. BE WAKENED. Be way-hay-hay-hay-HAKENED. Be way-hay-hay-hay-hay-hay-hay-HAKENED, be wakened, BE WAKENED, you shall be wakened, you sha-hah-hall be way-hay-hakened, you SHALL be wakened. You shall be WAKENED. You shall be wakened.'
Not much ambiguity there.

vii

People often question me about my association with Kreisler and ask for details. Kreisler I first met in a tiny Munich brauhaus in 1931. I was paring a drinkatif and looked up to find that the violinist had entered. There was nobody in the place but the two of us and since both were keenly interested in the violin, it was natural that we should (of all things) scrape up an acquaintance. (When a mutual acquaintance Zimbalist looked in later, we were so obsessed with this joke that we began to use our nails on him, explaining that we were merely scraping up an acquaintance.) But with Kreisler and myself, it was a question of close friendship from the start. The two men took an instantaneous liking to one another. The somewhat austere quality of Kreisler's mind found in my own intellect, chastened by a lifelong contemplation of human folly, the sort of *Kunstverstaendigkeit* that it sought, and the two men established a peculiarly happy relationship based primarily on mutual respect. Kreisler I found intelligent and talented, read in all the European literatures and a keen admirer of my own little thing (Leipsig, 1911) on Italian organ stops. Music, of course, we never discussed, but often after a long and exhausting evening on Hegel, we would find time to laugh at our serious-mindedness, take out the fiddles and scrape away for an hour or two at some duet or other of Corelli's. Kreisler sometimes would entertain me with a delicate cavatina on the landlord's saw, the return being an Irish hornpipe by myself.

I remember him calling to my rooms on March the 17th attired in tasteful kilts, a delicate compliment not only to me personally but to my country. We searched the town for the *schnapps* nearest to usquebaugh and spent a most enjoyable St. Patrick's Day. That evening I played for him the Schan Van Vocht, explaining that as might be gathered from the name, it referred to the life of an ancient German nobleman. He believed this until I enlightened him.

They were happy days. I wonder will they ever come again.

Reverie

I recall that we often discussed *perfection*. Was such a thing possible in man or his works? Was the pursuit of it a valid activity, granted that it cannot be attained? My own view was that man has made three things that are perfect – the sailing ship (well I remember them down at the point of the wall), the violin, mellow stradivarius acchord-aeon incapable of amelioration, and – O trihirundine ecstasy! – the drop of brandy.

Kreisler held that perfection was incompatible with art and would at once invalidate all art if once attained, the subtlety of art lying not in the attainment of perfection but in its indescribably diverse approaches to it.

viii

Research Bureau

Again keeping my promise (despite the fact that I gave it to you yesterday, strangely enough) I illustrate the apparatus perfected by the Research Bureau for cleaning dirty bottles.

It consists of a chain studded with knobs, spikes, and wire brushes, the whole being attached to a long wire handle. The chain is dropped into the dirty bottle, water is added and the bottle is corked. You then shake the bottle very vigorously, causing the spikes and knobs to scour every recess of the interior. The operation should not be undertaken late at night, as the noise is fearful. Also, if you are one of those persons who is convinced that it is all due to your stomach, please remember that the latter organ is much more intricate than a bottle and do not try to clean it out with this apparatus save under the supervision of a doctor. Many foolish persons have already swallowed several of these chains in a vain quest for health.

ix

Reading a newspaper recently I saw the heading THREE YEARS FOR MAN IN CUPBOARD. A stiff sentence, you will say, particularly since most people are unaware that it is illegal to enter a cupboard. Many eminent judges, however, have made it clear that they are determined to put down these cupboard offences.

The prosecution is always taken under certain old acts, Cap. xi, xviii and lvi Vic. Reg., generally cited as the Cupboard Regulation Acts. These somewhat obsolete statutes were later codified and brought up to date by the Presses Act of 1853 and further extended by the Small Presses Act of 1893. Grattan's parliament, a pioneer in certain matters, passed a Small Cabinets Act but this was quickly repealed after some eighty thousand pounds had changed hands in bribes.

The cupboard mania was a serious social problem a hundred years ago. It was quite common for an entire tribe of mendicants to live in the cupboards of a big house without the knowledge of the family occupying the house. These beggars would emerge at night, eat and drink everything in sight, and retire again, like ghosts at daybreak. A search of the cupboards rarely revealed any trace of the intruders: they were all expert carpenters and usually had constructed ingenious secret compartments, often with lifts and tiny stairways communicating with other cupboards. The wainscotting and underfloors of nearly all the grandiose piles of Victorian England were infested with beggars in the manner imitated by rats in our own day.

The Small Presses Act was intended to deal with a somewhat different problem. Dwarfs and undersized or deformed criminals realised the peculiar potentialities of their physique and took to infesting quite humble dwellings. The presses they entered were too small to admit of any structural alterations, but a system comparable to the jungle trick of camouflage was adopted. The intruder cunningly assumed the appearance of a roll of linoleum, a bundle of old clothing, a carpet bag, or whatever else looked appropriate to the setting. Cases came to light where dwarfs were sent to the laundry, passed through the machinery there, and returned to the householder neatly parcelled. A case was heard in 1893 in the King's Bench Division, in which a householder sued a steam laundry for the return of £48, being paid unwittingly over a period of twenty years for the laundering of a female dwarf. Held: that the laundry bills were well charged having regard to the fact that the company had laundered clothing for a fair consideration and was under no obligation, whether of statute or in equity, to satisfy themselves that the said clothing was not inhabited. Incidentally, a thorough search by the police of this householder's premises revealed a tribe of 18 foreign dwarfs complete with wives and children and accompanied by – of all things – a grotesque dog which had been trained to make himself look like an old cracked wash basin. There was a great to-do when these persons were charged in court. The learned judge created a scene on entering the court by ordering the attendants to clear away the litter of rubbish which he espied in the well of the court. He could scarcely be persuaded that this mass of old rope, buckets, lady's cycling bloomers and broken gramophones was in fact the defendants. When a cracked wash basin was led in growling loudly, his honour had to retire for a moment in order to recollect himself.

There were other odd cases. In Dublin it came to light that a somewhat overgrown dwarf who had once worked as a contortionist in the halls took to living in the press of a prominent gentleman's bedroom. This dwarf took the form of an old overcoat hung on a peg. Unfortunately, the gentleman one day lost his customary overcoat and perforce had to use temporarily the overcoat he had seen so often in the press. For a full week he paid his social calls attired in a middle-aged dwarf, whom he hung on hall-stands or handed to butlers.

Yes, much of the colour has gone out of life. Today nobody troubles to look even like a respectable Irish person.

X

Taking a solitary walk the other day, I found myself in the Ballyfermot direction and crossed that bridge, you know the one. I stopped to reflect, and in a moment my whole life had welled up in retrospect, the life of a steam man of the last generation. My lone fight for the full regulator in the teeth of the Dundalk shop bosses and the moguls in Design Room 2; my decision to go into the wilderness rather than concede what I chose to make my principles and rule of life; then recognition, fame and the dinner given to me in London by the British Union of Boiler Superintendents following the introduction to the steam world of my patent emulsion for treating dirty feed water. An irresistible urge came upon me to slip down the side of the bridge and walk the road. My conviction is that the Irish roads are not adequately walked, if in fact they are walked at all. I would be sorry to think that the road from Ballyfermot into the Inchicore yards had been walked in recent years by any decent steam man because 'bleeding' and 'rolling' could be observed at every step. Approaching Inchicore I gave a facetious hoot and after a short delay was accepted by the signal cabin. I steamed into a siding, reflecting that I had been entered up on the charts as a train.

I pottered about in the cold spring evening, watching inexpert shunters obsolescing the company's rolling stock and perpetrating outrages on small defenceless locomotives. Why cannot our men be sent to Swindon for a few weeks' training? Incidentally, I sheltered from the wind in the shade of a vehicle, took out my brandy-flask, had a slug and offered the flask to a man who was working on this vehicle. 'Sorry, I'm on the wagon,' was the reply I got. And well you may laugh.

xi

Those of us who were privileged to work with Clemenceau and L.G. in Paris after the last 'war' viewed with grave and increasing concern the growth of the hysterical national feeling which was to become so startling a feature of the succeeding years. We, who, at Versailles, had our fingers on the world's pulse, knew that this was a disquieting symptom of decay, a symbol of the organic dissension, the pathological individuality, which was to communicate itself from empires to nations, and from nations to the very families comprising them. We were universal doctors, pursuing a clinical science that was global; as such we were qualified to recognise in these dangerous Byronic outbursts the signs of occidental decomposition. It was, we said, the writing on the wall, but our voices were unheeded, and the aftermath is history.

The best prophets are subject to discouragement: for myself, I can say that I can see no justification for my 'life' if it be not such small services as I may have succeeded in rendering to poor suffering humanity. Even at this moment, my research organisation, financed wholly from my own pocket, is striving to devise the perfect alexipharmic for this dread disease, something that will give at least rest, if not the glimpse of happiness, to our tired human families of autochthonous chauvins. It is a task that must be pursued simultaneously in the medical, social and zoological spheres. It will be a costly and laborious task, requiring in its present stages skill, intelligence and fatiguing experiment, and, in the future, calling for the erection of many sanatoria throughout the world. But it must go on, nor can any civilised government afford to neglect it. Only posterity will know the value of this superhuman effort. But difficult as the task may seem, particularly in the regions of Mittel Europa, my own special interest and my particular assignment lies with the unfortunate brachycephalics of the westerly latitudes. My problem is how to help that person who, by birth or profession, is in the somewhat embarrassing condition of being an Irishman – that 'man' whose mortal ailment is not so much nationalism as nationality. Sometimes even I feel daunted, inadequate, afraid, in the presence of these herculean cares. Sometimes I feel that I am not sufficiently detached from the material upon which it is my vocation to work inasmuch as I am almost unique in the spheres of either journalism or science by reason of my own nationality. (I am 'Irish', you see.)

The problems which confront me cannot be solved without the cooperation and goodwill of my patients. Please, therefore – if you are Irish, write and tell me about it. Write frankly, secure in the knowledge that no eye other than my own will peruse your communication. Explain what it feels like to be Irish. State at what age you first realised that you were an Irish person. When did you have your first fight? At what age did you make your first brilliant 'Irish' witticism? At what age did you become a drunkard? Please tell me all, because there can be no cure until the pathological background has been explored. If you conceive yourself to be a cultural chauvin, please state whether your fixations are concerned with footballs, horses, folk dances, political frontiers or merely languages.

It is in your own interest to tell all. Remember that I too was Irish. Today I am cured. I am no longer Irish. I am merely a person. I cured myself after many years of suffering. I am sure I can help you if only you will have faith in me and write to me in confidence. Mark your envelope 'Irish' in the top left-hand corner.

xii

People who call to my place looking for advice on intimate problems often remark the bottle of Scotch whiskey which stands on my roll-bottom desk. I sometimes notice them covertly examining the 'whites' of my eyes and looking for tremors in my hands. Poor souls, they conclude that every man who keeps whisky (or even whiskey) in his house must necessarily drink it. Nothing could be further from the drouth. They should see me when, behind locked doors and alone, I uncork the bottle. Out comes the fountain pen and adroitly its little rubber stomach is filled with the yellow spirit. You see, most unambiguous of mortals, I like to write everything down in Black and White.

So much for my fountain pen. Please do not confuse it with my mountain pen on Ticknock. My mountain pen contains not whisky but decent black-faced sheep, all attired in exquisite woollies a present from Willie Dwyer. They all read the *Irish Times* and are frightfully loyal.

As for drink, they tell me it gives you a red nose, a complaint that can be passed on to your children. Damn nosa, how red it is!*

Damnosa haereditas: a blighted legacy.

xiii

Keats was once accosted in the street (it is unusual to be accosted in one's own house) by an acquaintance. This person asked for the loan of a fiver if you please. Keats noticed without any surprise that one half of the man's countenance was badly withered. 'You have a blasted cheek,' he said.

xiv

Do you ever stop to consider the nature of time (as the sarcastic Guard said to the publican caught pulling a pint at 10.40 p.m.). Look at it this way. Suppose a man's life is 60 years and a horse's 20. The horse is aging three times as fast as the man. This ratio is maintained in all propositions which involve the factor of time. When we talk of a horse galloping at 30 miles an hour, we mean that he is covering thirty miles in the space of a human hour. To assess the animal's performance objectively, we must think in terms of horse-hours. It takes him three of his own hours to cover this thirty miles and thus he is making the comparatively poor time of 10 miles an hour. On the other hand, a man running at the rate of ten miles an hour (and I did it myself back in '21) would be regarded as the fleetest of creatures by an elephant, who lives ten times as long as man, because the hour would represent only six minutes of the elephant's time. To give you some inkling of what's happening when a man travels at 'thirty' 'miles' per 'hour' *on horseback*, I'm afraid I would have to send up to Merrion Square* for the loan of a few quaternions (which I think are getting very scarce owing to the war. The visiting savants at the recent colloquium were warned one and all to bring their own and had to submit to some very ignorant cross-questioning by Customs people. Wearing apparel, forsooth! Bah!)

*Merrion Square contained the Institute of Advanced Studies, where the Nobel physicist Erwin Schrödinger was doing mathematical research.

XV

I have, as you know, a wide circle of friends. It is amusing to watch them when they gather in at night. Out comes the steel tape and the chalk and in no time they have the circle inscribed on the blue carpet. Then my priceless Sèvres chairs are placed round the circumference and there you are for the night – myself in the middle, a shy slight figure sitting on a stool in the blue kimono that is marked 'Palm Beach Sports Club' and the French pouring out of me like oil out of a mammoth Ploesti* gusher. At nine a plain meal of cocoa and hake is served, no table linen at all being used save my exquisite little mats of Chippendale lace. Supper over, I reach for my Guernerius a present from Kreisler and usually play an old Italian air. At ten to eleven – sometimes it is eleven or even later – I begin to froth at the mouth. My guests take this as a sign to withdraw. My wife then undresses me.

All my important decisions are taken in bed. I have, of course, been reading the newspapers in recent weeks and considering the tempo of events: I had no alternative at 2 a.m. on Wednesday last, but to make certain irrevocable determinations. The decisions recited below are announced and have immediate effect.

1. Lease of my villa at Ballybrophy must be determined, all pigs, horses and livestock to be disposed of by public auction; my nephew Reggie to have the Landseer and a choice of two objects from my collection of icons.
2. One of my flats in Paris (Département de la Seine) to be disposed of.

3. My subscription to the Knights not to be renewed and further pressure exerted on the Masons to get me into Guinness's, even as an assistant vat-house-overseer's greaser (£1,500 p.a. with apartments, light, fuel, medical attendance and two pints a day).
4. My agreement with the Bulgarian Secret Service to be terminated forthwith.
5. My frozen acids to be melted and offered to the Government for use in processes of urgent national importance.
6. In the event of my being got into Guinness's, application to be made to Kildare Street Club for membership on the grounds that I am a Southern Irish loyalist. (I am anxious to examine the window that was smashed by W. G. Grace with a slog to square leg from the Trinity playing fields in 1876.)
7. No more Gaelic nonsense.
8. My house in Lad Lane to be bought out before the Corporation gets after me for creating a nuisance. (I'll get rid of the animal all right but – I mean – how can people who have no capital to buy their houses outright be expected to expel the humble porker from the basement? How about the rint?)
9. Absolutely no more truck with Communists.
10. Retire finally from unequal struggle with railway cretins.
11. Get the wife into a home.

Eleven simple points for a new order of life. My idea is to become . . . . useful . . . . and good . . . . . and full of simple belief in humanity, a re-orientation of pig-breeding praxis, and the reform of our despicable monetary system. You see, I am thinking of becoming a reader of the *Standard*†.

---

*Ploesti: Oilfield in Romania.
†Defined elsewhere by Myles as 'a small pious weekly taken by the innocent to be the voice of the Catholic Church and as such profitably sold at church doors'.

xvi

I am, as you know, an Irish person and I yield to gnomon in my admiration and respect for the old land. Yet one tiny reservation. Do we, as a nation, treat our fellow-nations on this earth with the deference which is their due? Do we, I mean, vouchsafe them such little international courtesies as go to make a happier and a better world? Alas, I am not so sure that there we are entirely blameless.

Just one example. Consider the vast communion of asiatic agglomerates who live in the east, roguishly concealing their mysterious primal identities under the terminals U.S.S.R. By what courteous title are they called in the conversations of the Irish? They are called 'the Russian crowd'. Again, if one hears it said that 'your men across the way is putting up a fierce fight,' is one to infer that the feuds of local cornerboys have been thought worthy of discussion? Alas no. For here we have a reference to the British nation.

Is it enough, then, to be asked to be excused on the ground that we treat ourselves with courtesy as scant, being wont to describe the Oireachtas, which is the President and both houses, together with the entire Irish nation, its grandiose governmental dispositions, its artists, poets and armed forces, its staunch farmers and good families, as '*our* lads'? No, no, it is not enough that we do not, so to speak, shave unless we are going out. Our slovenly domestic manners must not be imported into our relations with other great peoples. Even if we did civilize them all and bring them the light of learning at a time when.

And nothing will induce me to comment on our custom of referring to our fellow-Irishmen in the far North as 'those —— —— above in Belfast.'

Footnote: I was at Clongowes with Metry – not Seán but the brother George. Good old Geo. Metry.

xvii

It so happens I don't smoke. Fifty years ago I was a holy show. Night and day never stopped. Tried everything – even travelling in Non-Smoking Compartments. No use, I was always thrun out at the next station. Bad, you will say, but of course you know much worse and I suppose you think I am going to stand here all day and listen to your dreary whines about the wife's sixty a day, sheets of bed perforated in fifty places if they're burnt in wan, ash everywhere, lights up in the middle of meals and so forth. Alas, I have heard it all too often. Bad all that may be but think of my own case – I was the most inveterate smoker in the you and I, Ted King (dumb) . . . . *and I wouldn't mind only never in my life did cigarette or heady meerschaum pass my lips!* I smoked like a chimney – too embarrassingly like. In those days it was unusual for a professional man (like myself) to venture 4th without glossy silk hat prime stop three coats best oil and four coats naphtha before fixing. But I may tell you that, at the wind-up, I didn't dare wear one. There were riots whenever I got out of my carriage in College Green to step into the Ould House, people didn't know what to make of it – the tall bearded figure in the grey frock coat bounding across the footpath with a dense black column of smoke pouring through the top of his silk hat. I tell you life was miserable for me the wife wouldn't have me in the house slept down there in the Inchicore sheds for years courtesy of the Directors (Reynolds* hadn't even been heard of in those days) and it was no picnic when I got an attack of downdraught (as I did more than once and – as it would happen – Henry Moore away in Galway). But after a while there I got on very well with the other decent patients, many of them victims of dread locomotive taxation. I took to puffing around the yards on my own and soon got into the way of things, learning to haul and shunt small local jobs gradually worked my way up triumph the night I dragged the mail down to Cork ten minutes ahead of schedule re-water at Mallow and stuck for twenty-three minutes on a side road to let Rafferty through with the night goods damn good going taking it all in all. And did this on my own steam I need hardly say. There is a new generation now of course, very few of the old crowd left. Very few of the young fellows that's going now knows what it's like to pull a train up hill and down dale for two hundred miles, half of them Irish miles. Very . . . . very . . . . few. And as cheeky as you like if you ask them to take a truck over to the Broadstone or bring a few of Goff's† horses as far as the Curragh of Kildare.

Yes faith. Sometimes I feel I am the only *real* steam man of the whole bunch. It so happens I don't smoke now . . . . much. The reason? The old story. The others were jealous of the good time I made. Turned the union on me. Was given my cards, past service forgotten, the fair weather friends were not long in showing their hand.

It's got to the stage now that if anyone says to me *Do you want a gnash tray* I get the idea they are insultingly offering me a receptacle for false teeth. Tiring if you like, boring, but in its own way rather tragic. For I too had my hopes. I thought at one time life was fair and that the race was to the free. Now I know better.

*A. P. Reynolds was Managing Director of the Dublin United Transport Company.
†Robert R. Goff & Co., the County Kildare bloodstock dealers.

xviii

That crowd above in Kildare Street* should take this Museum business a little bit more seriously. I glanced through there the other day and not an attendant in the place could show me the coffin. Gapes, and mouth hanging, and 'Whaaaaah?' One dolt even said: What coffin sir? I didn't lose my temper. 'Don't tell me,' I said with exquisite sarcasm, 'don't tell me you keep all those stones . . . . . in a . . . . glass case?' The same blank stare met me when I asked to be shown the chains. One fellow, more intelligent than the rest, hazarded the opinion that they might have been returnable under Article 10. If this is the case, it is a monstrous outrage. One ventures to inquire what action the so-called Fianna Fáil (!!!!)† Government has taken in the matter. I have not yet had an opportunity of going into the matter with Jack Costello‡ but I am certain that under the Statute of Westminster H. M. Government are bound to hand over to us in good condition the chains with which Ireland was bound. After that I was not surprised to find that of slumber's chains they haven't got a solitary link. How hurt poor gentle Tommy Moore** would be at this petty insult to his memory. No sign either of the gems she wore, not a peg out of the harp that once. Ha-ho, those wretched jacobins. Twenty years of serf-government (stet, by jove!) and not an attendant in the 'National' Museum can show me the true badge of nationhood! Ah, poor John Devoy!††

*Kildare Street contains the government buildings.
†Fianna Fáil: literally, Warriors of Ireland.
‡John A Costello (1891-1976) as Attorney-General had attended League of Nations and Imperial conferences.
**Thomas Moore (1779-1852), writer of 'The Gems She Wore' and other patriotic and romantic 'Melodies'.
††John Devoy (1842-1928), Fenian and patriot who died in America, alone, penniless and almost forgotten.

5
Montaignesque

In which Myles na gCopaleen comforts mankind by composing a decade of inspiring moral essays to cover all aspects of human nature and experience. In these important didactic works, which offer definitive precepts to follow in life, the humdrum encounters and random reading-matter of the philosopher as common man serve a binary purpose: to anchor the essayist's observations in the realm of la réalité, *while exploring the limitations of* la raison.

i

On Henry James

'How rarely,' says Mr Sean O'Faolain in the *Irish Times*, 'one hears the name, today, of Henry James.'

Fair enough. (Though around in my place, Mr O'F., the crowd often speak of him Tuesday evenings, few friends in for a glass of sherry and some dry chat.)

But my memory is as bad as the next. What actually was the name of Henry James? It's on the tip of my tongue. Shanachy or Shaughnessy or some name like that unless I'm very much mistaken. Willie James the brother I knew well.

ii

On Genius

The pint is raised, expertly tilted and a black torrent projected down past the inflamed tonsils. Moustache slowly patted with red spotted handkerchief. Leans back. Frightful stare from flat over-watered eyes. A slow heavy clank of chat follows: 'I . . . SEE WHERE . . . . A . . . . MAAN THERE SAYS . . . . GENIUS IS A . . . . . DISEASE . . . . . .' (Caesura: the audience is requested not to applaud between movements of the work.) *'Do you know what I'm going to tell you I've met a quare number of very very healthy men in me day.'* (Here there is a dry unlubricated laugh.) 'Aaah yes. There's very few afflicted that way round these parts very few indeed. Hah . . . .?' (Leans forward and taps out

charred contents of filthy pipe on your knee.) ' . . . . Aaand me
dear man the best of it is I wouldn't mind only . . . . .' the same
man goes on to say, Genius, says he, Genius, says he – listen till
you hear this, this'll give you a laugh – Genius, says he, *is much
rarer in women than in men.* Now isn't that a good wan? It's like
. . . luckit . . . it's like . . . . . it's like saying . . . . it isn't every
tailor can . . . . put a length of whipcord there on the table . . .
aaand cut you out a respectable hunting throusers . . . . . but the
threes the threes up there beyond the Twelfth Lock . . . . . *very
few of them can cut you a throusers at all!*

This monologue raises once again that profound and unde-
cided question – are women people?

iii

On Drama

And who said we don't know all about great plays? I hear where
Desire under the Ellimans* did very well this time. I'm not a bit
surprised. Sure . . . . sure Eugene listen to me Eugene MacNeill
that man is a pure genius . . . . . Ah yes. *Did you ever see Maureen
Becomes Electhric?* Oooooooooh, a . . . . . a . . . . . very lovely
thing a very lovely thing. Oh, if you haven't seen that I envy you,
me good man, I envy you, because you've got a great threat in
store (Raps counter, nods, mouthing at barman; index finger
indicates successively self and companion).

*Louis Elliman and his brother Maurice were among Dublin's leading
cinema and theatrical impresarios.

iv

On Music

One definitely *does* get tired of draughts. Not, of course, that
'game' with which chess-boards are occasionally defiled – one

does not get *tired* of that – and certainly not those small glass buckets of ruby-tinted lubricant, eightpence per go, which so often cause my Uncle Jim's stomach to gaze reproachfully up at the gullet orifice and say Do you know . . . there's a terrible draught coming from there!

No. I mean wind whistling in through the chinks of our interesting native concrete houses. They *can* be unpleasant. They *can* confer diseases of the respiratory system. Now attend please. The Research Bureau has been examining this problem and many years ago they established the great truth that there is no use in stuffing up a hole through which a draught is coming (whether with Caesar's head or otherwise) because *if you do it will simply come in somewhere else.* Very well. Now attend please. The Bureau has been trying to find how a draught may be harnessed to some useful task that will at the same time dissipate its pernicious energy. This task the Bureau has quite recently accomplished. The Bureau has devised a plan whereby *you can make your worst draught play the tin whistle for you* – and all in the privacy of your own home *with absolutely no scales, drudgery, practice or previous experience.* Nor need you know how to read a note of music. It is a discovery of great and lasting importance and I will try to explain it in simple unaffected non-technical language. Consider this illustration:

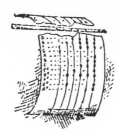

Obviously the first thing you must provide yourself with is a tin whistle. Three and ninepence is the controlled price, make certain that you don't pay more. The next thing you require is a roll of strong paper and certain little items of woodwork. (Attention, please – *all*.) Your next task is to decide upon a tune and unless I am mistaken in your sound outlook, it will be none other than Let Erin Remember. Very well. You must now carefully perforate your roll of paper so that when the tin whistle is blown, wind will be permitted to emerge through the reed appropriate to the note which is required. The frequency and duration of a note one secures by varying the dimension of the perforation in the paper. Next slide please.

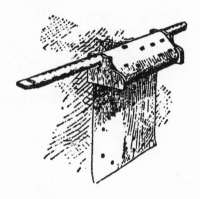

Here we have the finished article. Several tunes have been inscribed on the roll of paper and the little timber holder for the whistle and a winder have also been accurately constructed. One now attaches the end of the roll of paper to the winding roller and one connects the mouthpiece of the whistle to the aperture through which the draught is whistling by means of a delicate rubber tube. Now all is ready. One begins to wind and in a moment the high dulcet tones of Moore's immortal masterpiece have flooded the old-world room.

This is a thing that *is* worth trying. *Do* try it. The first time I produced the little apparatus in the presence of friends, they tittered and began to laugh. But when I began to wind, when the deathless strains of Beethoven's ninth violin concerto for piano and two organs began to flood the room . . . . .

I mean, why sit in draughts?

V

On Nobility

On the 21st of last month I saw this heading in the *Irish Times* – 'IRELAND IN NEED OF AN ARISTOCRACY.'

Yes, I agree. That is a real want; unquestionably one misses them. Take me for instance the whole business has left me . . . . nervous – you might say *lonely*. Really, I have lost my bearings. (It is not that I have lost my roots. What should I eat, they being lost?) As to whether the aristocrats have gone, doubt there cannot be. Let me tell you about my own case. I . . . . I . . . . I . . . . white-washed the place a few years ago. Nothing happened! Then, very quietly and unobtrusively, I . . . . renewed some of the thatch! Hardly seems possible but the thing escaped notice. Emboldened, I next induced my sleeping partner, gentlemanly person, cheque-book at disposal on quarter-day, takes quite a load off my shoulders, I – this seems horribly ungrateful – I . . . . induced him to sleep . . . . outside! He . . . . grunted somewhat at the idea of removing his essentially pink hairless person from my couch. Not a word from the Big House. Then, I simply grew reckless. Fellow I know – he's a writer – I had him write *my* name *in Irish* on my cart! *I got away with it!* Finally . . . . plucked up all my courage . . . . *washed myself*! (Could have sworn I had gone too far.) Well. it's absolutely incredible but the rent remains exactly *as before*! The bailiff? I literally haven't seen him for years. Everything seems so unreal, so . . . . so . . . . un-Irish, one simply sits in a daze from day to day living in the same cottage and *never being evicted*! (As for invitations to dance for the aris-

tocracy after the claret with my boots bound with straw . . . .
they are a thing of the past. It's hard to explain these cruel snubs
to a man of my age.)

vi

On Xenophon

One cannot be up to some of these shop-keepers. Went into a
Gross Herr the other day and ordered some jam. After a lot of
humming – accompanied, indeed, by that essentially High
Court activity, hawing – he agreed to meet my wishes in the
matter of greengage jam with only purest fruit juices added. I
courteously put down my money and waited. And that'll be
another threepence, the ruffian added, for the pot. Am I to
understand, I remonstrated sternly, that you are prepared to
sell me this jam on condition that I also buy another article, to
wit one porcelain pot made in Belgium value one penny far-
thing?

Fearful row. Apparently I was taken for an inspector from the
Department of Irish Sweepstakes, Ballsbridge. The frightened
man rushed back into the dwelling house part of his premises
whence I could hear him shouting to his wife to bury the four
bicycle tyres in the garden and to get the stuff in the loft out by
the back door. When he came back he explained that most
people preferred to buy their jam in pots rather than 'loose' and
that he was only facilitating the public, he had a blameless
record save for an incident in 1927 when, in his absence at a
funeral an assistant, since dismissed, had contrary to his express
orders, served an old lady with a bottle of stout for consumption
on the premises –

'I prefer my jam loose,' I said coldly. I was in a bad temper
and was determined to make an issue of this.

'Will you take it in your pocket sir?'

'Yes.'

Well, there it was, had to stand there like a fool while a pound of this green mess was shovelled into one of my pockets. So foul my temper when I got home that the nearest thing to hand, a valuable volume of Xenephon, was torn to shreds in an endeavour to . . . . carry out a disengaging action. Rueful to recollect Cicero – if one recollects aright – *Libri Xenophontis perutiles sunt ad multas res*, the books of Xenophon are useful for many things.

vii

On the Artist

It seems I must resume my little war against a certain apostrophe. A Saturday or two ago we had Mr Edward Sheehy writing in the *Irish Times* about Harry Levin's book on James Joyce. Twice we have a reference to 'Finnegan's Wake'. How often have I made it clear that this will not do? The title of the book is 'Finnegans Wake' and there is no apostrophe.

'The nature of the contemporary situation,' the reviewer says, 'is not clear, here or anywhere; less here, I should say, than anywhere. And any tyrannical attempt to clarify it by compelling it, in theory, to assume a particular ideological pattern, makes it still less clear. If we are to clarify it at all, we must do so by learning from the artist who has suffered its contradictions, inanity, dishonesty and futility in himself.'

Alas, this will never do either. Imagine anyone reading Mr Joyce in order to clarify the contemporary situation – or clarify anything! One should remember that the great artistic feats accomplished in medieval times were carried out by people who conceived themselves to be decent workmen, people who simply did not know how to do a bad job. On Sundays they put on their best clothes and went to Church. Nowadays your 'artist' is a neurotic imbecile; he has the cheek to discern in his own dementia the pattern of a universal chaos and it is no coincidence that most of his books are dirty and have to be banned. Beware of 'culture', reader; of 'art' and 'artists' be careful and apprehensive. Such things were very fine when they came out first, they were part of the commonplace shape of life and nobody could possibly take exception to them. But when isolated in our own day to become merely a self-conscious social cult, an excuse for all sorts of bad behaviour, a pretext for preciosity and worse – know then that words like 'culture' and 'art' do not mean what they meant. One great danger is this: if we admit that an artist is necessarily neurotic, many neurotic poor souls will conclude that they must be artists. And that is not an attitude that should be encouraged, however much it may float our poor country out into the main stream of European culture. It cannot be too strongly stressed that a true aesthetic perception is part of the essential equipment of mankind and when one nowadays meets an oddly-shirted gossoon who blathers self-consciously about 'art', one sees at once that he is a deficient type, one who has receded from the primitive norm. The instinct for propriety and beauty is highly developed even in animals. Hens, for example, are skilled in the plastic arts and can produce works of art that are not only impeccable in design and delicately coloured, but edible. The bee produces – albeit by a process that seems unnecessarily complex – an exquisite yellow and nourishing mess, faultlessly packed and ready for market. I do not find, however, that either the hen or the bee, by reason of mere mastery of a particular art-form, claims to be entitled to clarify the contemporary situation. The truth is, of course, that no such clarification is possible, nor is the word 'contemporary' of any significance. The essentials of life do not – indeed cannot – vary from one century to another, for life itself means reproduction and repetition; to hold otherwise is to confuse life itself with the temporary vessels which contain it very temporarily.

People who call to my lodgings for advice often ask me whether being Irish is itself an art-form. I am not so sure that the answer can here be yes. One asks oneself whether the state of being Irish is characterised by the three essential requisites of

James Aquinas Joyce – *integritas, consonantia, claritas.* This
question each one of us must answer for himself, first looking
into his own heart. It would save so much trouble if we could all
answer in the affirmative. 'Paudrig Crohoore, R.H.A.' would be
a grand way out; that each citizen should at birth be acknowl-
edged to be an artist would save us all a lot of trouble and
embarrassment.

viii

On Drink

Those of us who spend all our time in public houses are often
puzzled by pronouncements made by the Irish Association for
the Prevention of Intemperance . . .

What!

Yes, I *do* spend all my time in a public house. You see (smirks
primly and rubs incredible lobe on ear) you see . . . I own one.
Have to be there to dish out the liquor. But as for touching
it . . . . ! (Throws hands wildly in air in theatrical gestures of
renunciation.)

To comb Bach, however.

The Irish Association for the Prevention of Intemperance is
continually denouncing 'the cocktail habit'. The IAPI (to
abbreviate in a rather north-westerly Greek way this non-
beered, spiritless and unsherried body) suggests that many
catastrophes have their guinnesses sorry genesis in the consumption of cocktails on the part of young women. Now this
is simply not true. I issue a (raspberry) cordial invitation to Mr.
Christy Reddin of the Licensed Vintners' Association to bear
me out on this – on the strict understanding, however, that he
carries me in again. *Nobody drinks cocktails nowadays.*
Through their eccentric refusal to enter pubs, the IAPI are
twenty years out of date in their conception of the squaw
liquor ritual. Nor is it clear that they quite know, or ever knew,

precisely what the cocktail is. One feels that they single it out for obloquy because of its vaguely decadent and American ring – like foxtrot and cakewalk. Actually the cocktail is high up among the more harmless alcoholic compounds. It is a 'long drink'; its base is usually a little gin, but this is overwhelmed by a vast addendum of soda, fruit flavourings, ice and the like. It is the cynical answer we publicans give when we are asked to serve little girls. We are married men ourselves, the two daughters are in Eccles Street, and we will in no circumstances be a party to anything approaching real puellate carousing. We fake up this essentially coloured and bubbling mess and serve it piping cold. Nor do we stop there. We know the whole thing costs us about tenpence but by way of teaching the moustachioed whippersnapper who brought her in a lesson, we ask him to pay us two shillings and eightpence for the dose which, with fourpence for his own glass of plain, makes it three bob for the round.

There is, moreover, no such thing as 'the cocktail habit'. Any lady really interested in alcohol sees through this sham in about a month and begins to insist on her share of the malt. If her choice still be cocktails, she is no drinker and if the IAPI approached this drink problem scientifically, they would carry out a great campaign for the revival of the cocktail fashion. (Blows nose and slumps forward meditatively.) Though . . . . though in a way . . . . the language would be an easier job . . . .

(Goes out of room thoughtfully and comes back with small faded photograph in florid gilt frame.)

Do you . . . do you see that? That was taken in 1924. Yes, semi-frock-coat, stove-pipes an' all – that's me. And this extraordinary person in the hat, apparently attired in a plaque of symmetrical cardboard, hapless, hipless and hopeless? The wife, of course. You wouldn't remember the twenties, of course, but it was all cocktails then, and the Charleston, and cottages up on Ticknock an' poretry, and your two men opening the Gate Theatre. Will I ever forget 'Ghosts' in the

Peacock? And poor A.E.! (Begins to blubber quietly.) And the games of chess we used to play in the old D.B.C. in Dame Street! (Produces small capsule of 'snow' from vest pocket and takes enormous dose; waddles out of room to replace picture, crying and snuffling audibly. Without, voice can be heard muttering:)

Cocktails, is it? *Cocktails!* Ah, God be with the days!

ix

On Independence

A correspondent wrote this in a Sunday paper recently:

> I wish to protest at what I consider a deliberate insult to our National Anthem, and incidentally, to the whole Irish nation, by a body of musicians who performed in one of our Dublin halls during the past week. They omitted to play the Anthem, either prior to or at the conclusion of their concert at the Metropolitan Hall.

Hmmmmm.

I suppose one should be thankful that they were not guilty of the unbelievable solecism of failing to play the tune before or after the concert. This sort of thing amuses me. By which I mean, of course, that it makes me very very angry. The veins on my neck bulge. Since when, I shout, did the playing of this poor tune make or unmake this most historic and loyal Irish race? Who gave this boy authority to receive insult on behalf of 'the whole Irish nation'?

We have, of course, no national anthem, the thing has no constitutional or statutory sanction and as I understand the laws of the humble community in which we live, a body of musicians may or may not play the air, according as they wish.

But I regret very much that when this state was being founded and fitted out with its civil accoutrements, steps were not taken to stamp out the craving for a 'national anthem'. The 'national anthem' is a characteristically imperial pomp and whatever utility the device may have for use abroad when an Irish team may win a soccer match, or the like, why this inexcusable fashion of playing it – or eight bars from it – every night at home? Why must this Irish nation so continually salute itself?

We are very unenterprising copycats if you ask me. We could well drop a lot of this self-conscious state finery, disband our ruritanian hussars, stop stealing the Guinness trade mark as the national monogram, and . . . . hmmmmm . . . . completely forget about printing the titles of our newspapers in a phoney gothic script as foreign to this country as I am myself. There is greater enterprise in walking naked. Another thing we insist on having – simply because other countries have it – is a civil service. Moreover, our civil service is quite the conventional kind; it is above reproach and it is discontented. The members thereof have 'grievances'. Not for worlds would we dare have a corrupt and profligate civil service. 'Finance' (as the grim arbiter of all Irish destiny is called) would not hear of such a thing. We are civilised, you see. Our boast is that we produce the finest horses, the finest whiskey, the finest heifers and the finest higher executive officers in the world. To the *Statist* we have given hundreds of editors. Even to the *Irish Times* we have given editors. Keep this under your hat but the Editor of the *Irish Times* is . . . . Irish! Owing to physical propinquity of two islands destinies inextricably intertwined, commonwealth of nations, futility of dwelling on history, promotion of amity and goodwill, tongue that Shakespeare spoke, our indefeasible claim to a seat at the peace conference. Ha-ho.

I hold also that Irish lord mayors, as a class, are essentially inadmissible. Blushing self-conscious foreignism never went further than that institution. Why you Irish can't just be Irish and leave it at that beats me. Why you must so raffishly ape alien citizenries defeats me. Why at the same time you exclude so rigorously what is admirable in other civilisations agonises me. Some of you would deprive me even of my English language! Really often wonder are the Irish people really worthy of Trinity College.

X

On Nationality

Or look – take the case of that distinguished nobleman, My Lordship. We have lived our life with dignity, refraining always – with that exquisite sensibility that is so particularly *ancien régime* – from the enormous gaffe of living someone else's life. We have tasted to the full the suites of experience (believe us, mahogany is not what it used to be and there is a class of greenhart going around now that wasn't heard of in your father's day . . .), known the poignancy, neigh! . . . love, in many an outlandish port, drunk the cup of pleasure to the drugs, I beg pardon, the dregs, ate fried hare off gold platters in the royal establishments of the Indian Empire. True, in the muddy waters of politics we have not soiled our thin blue-veined hands since that terrible night in '22 when, outraged but calm, we stalked goutily out of the Rump Parliament. (Next day, of course, the iniquitous Reform Act became law, haven't spoken to H.M. since.)

Life, however, has been graciously accepted, and fortified with the right of seigniory, three or four bins of that claret, some excellent sack, our railway director's travel pass, and the few suave, indispensable vices that make maturity supportable, one has continued in the mellow grandeur of senescence, to carry still the horn for one's pack, to take the highest fence without fear, to flog unmercifully the loutish yokels who drive crude ploughs under one's very horse's hooves, and even to permit the rascally attorney who wears our old suits to came to infamous 'arrangements' with the garlic-scented jacks-in-office who would fain plunder from us the few pitiful rents that remain.

One learns nothing, one forgets nothing. Of horseflesh one is still a judge; for a pretty woman there is no gallantry of which we hold ourselves incapable – and damn the one of them can resist our trim military presence, our aura of deeds in the eastern deserts, our lofty dissolute air. (I say nothing of our lofty dissolute heir.) And always, those clever clever trousers, fabricated in one piece by a morose gothic artist, of nationality Italian yet a London person by choice of residence – a specialist in picturesque ruins. By Appointment H.M.

That then is the picture. Who shall wonder if such a figure, the wise accomplished polyglot who has carried himself (and sometimes the jarvey) with much distinction in the chancelleries and courts of the known world, is courted by his peers and vassals alike for his wit, his charm, his multilingual fluency, his brilliant, coruscating, essentially wearisome conversation? And yet . . . and yet, though it is true that I have the entrée (and sometimes the hors d'oeuvre) to the best houses in all the capitals of the globe . . . yet, how shall I put it? . . . here in Dublin, where, for example purely for the sake of the staff the house in Great Charles Street is still kept open year in year out . . . here . . . here . . . *I am not welcome.* Ça . . . ça . . . c'est tout à fait égal, v'savez . . . mais . . . to be told by one's own tenants that one is not Irish because one does not speak Irish . . . to be told that to be Irish one has to reject . . . foreign cultures . . . and live as our Irish ancestors did, fishing, praying and abstaining from drink . . . !

You see (and I have said this before) I never asked these people who shout at the corner of Abbey Street to regard me as Irish and to be denied an uncoveted honour is to be assessed as the peer of one's boggish interlocutors. We conceive ourselves not of Irish, English, French or Norwegian sucklings. We are merely the ageless gentleman who has encountered and outgrown all nationalities, swallowed the oyster which was our world, cheapened for ourselves eternally this demi-paradise.

Montaignesque

We are . . . ourselves . . . a small personal nationality. Put it
another way . . . Sinn Féin.

6
Urgent Ministry

In which Myles na gCopaleen returns from France (or other summer resort) in combative, even bellicose, mood. Certain serious matters must be attended to at once, on both home and global fronts: most pressingly, Ireland needs to be redefined. But it seems that the world may be turning a deaf ear to his teachings, and his enemies are mustering.

i

Ah! Good morning! (Shuffles in, places cheap cardboard attaché case on floor, walks instantly to 'sideboard' to check whiskey and sherry stocks; not satisfied because mere volume is intact, tests whiskey with hydrometer. Rings bell. When squaw-wife appears, embraces her distastefully, rubs hand on own stomach, throws back head showing 'whites' of eyes. Comprehending wife departs to prepare rashers and eggs.)

Well!

How good to be back! How good to be in Arnott's* – sorry, in harness – once more! To have defeated those who wish me ill, to have confounded my enemies, to be in position to resume again my leadership of this Irish people – that . . . . . that . . . . is comforting. It augurs well for the past.

When I was jailed by the secret police for my principles, I think I am entitled to say – while I am neither brave Mahon nor cow-herd – that I would not talk and gave my captors no satis-faction. I am in nowise ashamed to admit that I have been in what one may call the *cruiskeen*. Let the truth be told, ruat column. Nearly all distinguished Irishmen have been in jail at one time or another – some as prisoners, others as warders; one or two, indeed, as governors. A man must have the courage of his convictions.

A funny thing – in my case my health gave way after a short time. A Corkman doctor ordered me to de (sic) bay. My dis-order was first thought to be lead poisoning, but I instantly rejected this diagnosis. I was the worst in the world, of course, but further tests showed that I was suffering from a severe attack of . . . . penicillin. (!!!!) We got the aga cooker going in no time, and soon we had baked a blanket of anti-toxic plasma – the only *safe* way to counter this new peril. I cannot say that I was discharged cured. Cured I was but they could not discharge me until the sentence imposed by the beaks had run its course (of all things).

I have not, of course, seen a paper for weeks but odd (even even) snatches of conversation in the exercise yard gave me to understand, in no unambiguous manner, that in the absence of the cat, mouse-play has not been wanting. *Parturiunt montes* – and the same mountains were, at the time of my departure, mere molehills. *They will not get away with it.* Over each back number I will go, nothing will remain unchallenged; all – *all* – will be exposed. (Leans forward, with tongs picks copy out of heap of back numbers on floor. Spreads it open on floor.) Take this absurd letter, for instance, written by some knave skulking behind the cloak of anonymity: indignation was the key-note, high was the time, grave, by implication, the alleged scandal:

A short time ago the writer observed on the waste land situated at Loughlinstown, Co. Dublin, a living mass of rats, numbering about 1,000, feeding at their leisure . . . .

Living mass of rats, eh? Did the writer then expect to see a thousand dead rats feeding at their leisure . . . . . . even in Loughlinstown? And does he suggest that they should bolt their food and have their digestive systems in the same condition as, say, my own? Why can't people leave rats alone? All they ask is to be left in pies.

That, of course, is only a tiny matter. (Pokes with tongs.) Other things have been said and written. Hmmmm. Bernard Shaw. Picasso. The Abbey, last resting-place of Goldsmith and Doctor Johnson, has been attacked and besmirched. An *Italian*

134

writes to say that *Ireland* is, and has been for years, in a deplorable condition.

I fear there is much stern work ahead. (Throws down tongs, begins to take off coat.) Come back tomorrow – all.

*Arnott's: *Not* the famous Grafton Street department store – Sir John Arnott had been a celebrated Managing Director of the Irish Times Ltd.

ii

Mr Nichevo*, the writer on my left (your right) is continually saying things that are at once puzzling and hurtful. He is the strangest man in the ephemeral world of journalism. (I say nothing of the diurnal world of ephemeralism.) For example, heaven knows what he has today but the other Saturday he had a paragraph headed CHAOS ON THE QUAYS. Efficient, if you like – quite good, in fact. But such waste! Why not simply QUAYOS? (Nobody ever asks my advice until it's too late.) He continues:

'In one of the queues I espied the forlorn figure of my friend Sean O'Faolain, Editor of the *Bell*, and one of our foremost literary men . . . .'

How odd that Mr O'Faolain was located merely in . . . . *one* of these queues! And why . . . . why am *I* not mentioned in that sentence? Am I . . . . . *nobody*? Surely if one is writing of literary men, in common manners one should mention the name of the greatest one of all?

And imagine getting the words 'forlorn' – not to say 'Faolain' – and 'Bell' into one sentence! The damn literary . . . . Keatness, sorry, cuteness, of it!

*Without recourse to ancient calendars, we may deduce that this is a Saturday, for it was then that 'Nichevo' (the Editor himself, R M Smyllie), wrote.

135

iii

Most extraordinary thing. A person unknown to me has written a letter as follows:

> I think you are very sound on the Vocational Report and read your column every day with much interest and enjoyment. It happens that I do some writing myself and I enclose some verses (humorous?) which may be of interest.

There must be some mistake. Sometimes I wonder do people really *understand* my instructions as issued from time to time. (Presses buzzer. Bank porter comes in with tray full of stout and oysters.) Thank you, leave them on the piano. It is a strange thing. Why do people want me to . . . . *like* their comic verses? Why do they shamble and prance around their temporary part-time world, grinning and telling stories I am expected to think funny? Why am I pestered with offers of marriage by persons who represent themselves (by post) to be titled, moneyed, beautiful and amiable? I ask these questions but I take no interest in the answers. I do not trouble to observe the rather tawdry terrestrial impedimenta which surround me. Emotionally, the 'world' gives me nothing; intellectually it is of no assistance. I am on my way out, that is all. The work which I came here to accomplish is well in hands. It is not to be thought that any . . . mortal 'activity' can affect the success of this transcendant enterprise; it is not to be assumed that I am a passenger – and how much more improbable that I should be, say, a member of the team, *or* the navigator! I am . . . . call me an Inspector, an Ambassador, a Plenpotentiary without Portfolio if you will – *but* . . . . . . understand without ambiguity that my terms of reverence (yes, reverence) are not capable of enduring human scrutiny, my mission and its manifold implications find their raison d'être in a realm which cannot be apprehended in the 'light' of sense-experience, my presence here is a 'phenomenon' so completely outside and beyond the planes of existence which human thought is able to hypothesize into the structure of the universe that – considered in 'relation' to that presence – the whole monster procession of life can only be understood as a sort of epiphenomenal magic lantern show, too dim, too dull, too intolerably indistinct to amuse even the most backward, the most barbarous, of infants.

That is the picture. I am the shadow on the wall of the cave mentioned by Plato. I am the second one from the left in the grey frock coat and dundrearies. My wish is that I should not be disturbed. Please do not speak to me. I appear, perhaps, to make requests, to ask favours, to issue commands? This is a misunderstanding. I ask for nothing. These be the merest ghost imperatives – they are the expression not of the gross, unsublimated, merely human will, but of wisdom, humility, holiness, greatness, the projection temporally of qualities unfamiliar even to the dead and the unborn. (I have, I warn you, been both and speak on this difficult matter with authority.) With myself and certain other orientals, person-ation is a profound philosophic . . . . phase, *not* simply a traditional method of recording votes. So that when I say: Do not greet me in the street – it is not the negative order it appears to be, but rather the first ingrown intonation of a maximal doxology, the first intimation of an eschatological New Deal, the first ritual session of the pan-hibernian cult of claustrotheosis. That is all. (Pours stout into wash-hand basin, empties oysters in beside them, starts to stir mixture with old slipper.)

And one other thing. I am not a vocational group, do not wish to be organised or become 'functional', in no circumstances will I join a trade union. The reason? Because I am, myself, a . . . . a . . . . vocation.

iv

Chapman once spent a long holiday in Conamara and returned with health completely shattered. To Keats, who visited him in hospital, he explained that he was forced night after night to attend certain not uncheerful requiem vigils and that in practice this meant subsisting for weeks on a diet of poteen and plug tobacco.

'The West,' Chapman murmured wanly, 'seems to be a place concerned solely with nocturnal preparations for funerals.'

'The West's a wake,' Keats said drily.

v

Sometimes I get discouraged. I *try*, mind you, to get this old land of yours run according to some rational plan. My directions, suggestions, hints are ignored.

Take the E.S.B., for example. They have put out a report about the electrification of rural Ireland. They do not hesitate to reprove the farmer who milks his cows otherwise than by electricity. They suggest that mangolds should be mashed electrically. They think it is silly to have oil lamps in the haggard.

That is fair enough. But will it be credited that this same Board's own 'station' at the Pigeonhouse, Dublin, is run – not electrically – but on steam!

Or again – take the Dublin Transport Company. On one plea or another they have failed to provide a shelter for intending passengers at the Nelson Pillar. The unfortunate people must queue in the rain. Probably quite a few get pneumonia and die from this exposure. The 'brains' behind this concern apparently do not realise that there is already a very fine shelter at this spot, one that could be used until a more suitable one is erected. I refer, of course, to the Nelson Pillar. There is no reason in the world why people should not queue up – and it would be 'up' for once – inside the pillar. The queue would be corkscrew-wise and vertical – but it would be dry. One would know readily – from a glance at the file of people out on the platform – when to give up and call a taxi. The company should be pilloried for their obtuseness in this matter.

vi

You may have overlooked a paragraph in this paper the other day under the heading 'Smugglers Smelled.' Two men were nabbed.

'Preventive Officer Dunne stated that, as they smelled strongly, he took them from the train at Goraghwood, and, on being searched, the sausage casings were found wound round their bodies and legs.'

Most people would be facetious about a paragraph like that – talk about black and white padding (stet), one man being rasher than the other, and soforth. I suppose it *is* funny to be wearing sausage-casings. But what struck *me* about the item was the extraordinary jingle 'found wound round'. It is a piece of English that looks, sounds and smells like a trisected sausage.

Eccentric Islanders

Another paragraph you probably *did* notice was headed ARAN ISLANDERS WANT DECENT LIVELIHOOD. Unlike whom? Is this 'news'?

vii

Impatience – indeed any of the human petulances – I know to be silly. These imperfections do not exist in any of the other existences. But confining (for the moment) my remarks to this terrestrial scene, it can be said for impatience, silly though it be, that it is a quality, an activity, that is shared with humans by those wiser folk, the animals. Of silliness itself, this cannot be said.

Very well. (Suddenly leaves room, shouts downstairs to wife to go to Vincent's* to get her sore neck dressed. Returns fondling scrofulous cat. Resumes.) Very good. Will it be wondered at then that even I was tempted to some small gesture of impatience – a shrug, an exasperation of the lips – when in this newspaper the other day I read the headline

DANGER OF THIRD WORLD WAR

Which of ye will rebuke me for that temptation to be untrue to those terrene-housed spiritual agglomerates which, for the want of a better term, I call MYSELF? I have lived in Europe all my life. I have spent many years in Tibet, in Syria, in Iceland, in Guatemala. I am an old man and have devoted all my life, all my energy, all my money to the service of humanity, keeping back nothing of wisdom, of charity, of wealth which might benefit. My ancestors, of whom there were thousands in every age, have been statesmen, lawgivers, philosophers, priests, not less distinguished than they were pious, diligent, honourable, and fearless in the defence of truth. I have known war and I have known peace. I have seen the splendour of the Pax Romana, yet have known its servitude; I have witnessed in war prodigies of valour, selflessness and human dignity, yet have never blinded myself to its squalor, the deformed soldier, the outraged civilian, the destruction of household gods and everything that . . . . little folk hold dear. It has been my sublime privilege over the course of the last ten centuries to see unfolded the fantastic pattern of human destiny; little has escaped my notice – granted that I am – if archetypal, human. Yet even now I feel (in a real sense, transcending the cheap vaudeville of the Yogi) that I am but trembling on the *limen* of knowledge. I am saying these things, not out of vainglory – that were too funny – but rather that ye may see, may understand, may benefit when I explain the

pathetic grossness of this . . . . this . . . . DANGER OF THIRD
WORLD WAR.

You see, there is in things an eternal dichotomy, a conflict
of concepts within the orbit of the one great concept, a terrible unity that is achieved only by the fusion of
irreconcilables, and the very outline of which – alas! – though
we may guess at it – is, and must remain, imperceptible to us.
Thus 'black' is the opposite of 'white' – I use inexact terms
simply for the purpose of exposition – and its very blackness
is inapprehensible if we were not aware of the concept
'white'. Love, the great life-principle, is incomprehensible
knows one not hate. Earth and water subsist jointly in this
irrevocable dualism. We Europeans, we of the great creative
races, we Jewish people, for us history holds no surprises, the
sun shines on no novelties, death holds no terrors; we are not
aware of 'dangers'. One does not speak of a 'Third' world
war. War does not cease with your armistices – nor is peace
initiated. War is no accident – either in the bulgar sense
(meant vulgar but how futile to change now), or in the sense
that it could be a property not essential to our conception of
the substance, man. War is to be understood only in terms of
man; man only in terms of war. There is no third war. There
is only one war and to think that it will cease within the
bournes of humanity's tenure of the soil is to think as one
thought in the nursery, so very long ago, in Asia Minor.

And that will be all for today.

*Hospital.

viii

We are now entered into the murk of autumn. I do not apprehend this fact by espying the customary carpet of brown loaves
(nay, leave it, printer – it is a pretty image of yours) as I ride in
the bois. The fact is that the Knights are drawing in, now is cur-

tain close drawn, now doth the viper tongue renew his talent. For truth to tell, the customary autumn campaign of whispered calumny and detraction directed against my person by beings eaten up by self-interest has again opened up. I am not unaware of what these creatures say, not ignorant that they have launched an attack, as baseless as it is dastardly, on the good name and reputation of my family.

The Irish people will by now be well aware of the custom, observed scrupulously by me over the last couple of decades, of studiously ignoring the cowardly and bullying menaces of the hired thugs and desperadoes, commissioned – nay, even equipped with cudgels – by parties in high places to reduce or to endeavour to reduce by every means in their power, be these fair or fowl, the spirit, the high courage and resolve which none can attempt to deny have always characterised not only my public life but my conduct of those more personal affairs where honour, delicacy and the sanctity of the home tend rather to be luxurious pleasures than the stern duties they inevitably become when applied to the conduct of affairs of state.

Just men throughout the length and breadth of this fair land must know how consistently I have wrapped the incorruptible flame of my probity and virtue in a mantle of unaffected indifference; all must bear testimony to the unassailable quality of my conduct throughout these years. But, in spite of obvious temptations, I have always refused to regard myself as being other than ordinary flesh and blood; I have conceived this foible to be my right and my privilege, small guerdon for my not inconsiderable services to the dear land of my adoption – and so, the time has come when my mere human nature asserts itself so strongly that I can no longer pretend not to be affronted. I can no longer stand calmly by. Insults levelled at myself must, I hold, of their very nature be false and ridiculous. But offence offered to my family is another matter and I have the humility to regard it as a matter even graver. This then is the occasion when I no longer choose to disdain the challenge, to reject the smarting affront of the caitiff's glove, to deny myself, to deny the shades of those who have gone before me, the satisfaction of entering the lists to break a lance in a cause which I am pleased to regard as being lofty, worthy, and glorious. My people have settled in this town of Dublin (and I do not exclude the financial connotation of 'settled') for the past four or five centuries, but that is not to say that the unity of the family, the close association with our cousins the Gaplinsteins in Luxembourg, with the Sicilian Marchese Coplinino, the duc de St. Gauplain in Caen, the Earl of Cruiskness and Ilawn in Scotland and the Duke of Copeland in England – that is not for a moment to suggest that the close communion has ever for a moment been disturbed. We are all part of the one great, European family – our common ancestor we hold to be that stalwart hero of pre-Imperial Rome T. Coplinius Miles four times consul seven times censor and subsequently, with his uncles Romulus and Remus, deified under the Emperors. The exploits of collateral branches of the family under the Comnenan dynasty, with the Ming people, with Genghis Khan, with Ivan the Fourth, these are details which must await their due meed of praise in another place and at another time. But that, in brief, is the story of my family. What then can I say about the muttered accusation which was brought to my ear last Friday, that my grandfather's people – forsooth! – were tinkers in the Liffey valley?

I can but cry: It is a lie, my lords, and I do not for a moment hesitate categorically to stigmatize it as such. These boys were not tinkers – they were thinkers.

Of my link with The Great O'Neill, more anon.

ix

I continue to see puzzling statements in the papers. Extraordinary what they print sometimes. (Fallacy: papers do not print, they are printed upon. Please note.) Here, for instance, is a heading we had the other day:

CYCLIST WEDS

News? Faith then I can't see it. Why, pray, should cyclists not wed? Is there something in the exercise of the craft, some secret vow, some occult commitment that makes the founding of a family, the cultivation of the sweet domestic arts, the cherishing of womankind (aplurally) incompatible with cyclism? Are we to infer, forsooth, that there was never any Mrs Sturmey Archer? I am not a journalist, of course (I am a philosopher) and perhaps it is presumptuous of me to expect to comprehend newspapers.

X

An Old Time Graduate

Talking of what one reads, I saw recently – could it have been in *Pravda*? – a piece about barytes: the writer mentioned that it is being mined 'on the slopes of Yeats's Ben Bulben . . .'

Only one error in that statement – the word is *bawytes*. (It is an anagram on the name of its inventor, Dr W. B. Yeats.) As to poor Bulben, I knew him well. He was a B.A., H.Dip. in Ed., and joined the Keating Branch in October, 1903, same year as myself. He was one of the best, R.I.P. People of an older day will remember the brother Hugh Bulben ('Hughie'), later to find fame as Chief Mechanical Engineer, Ceylon State Railways. I understand that Supt. Bulben, G.S., now stationed in the south, is a cousin. Eheu!

xi

The Oireachtas* is in full swing. It is supported by considerable manifestations of step-dancing, pipe-playing, kilt-wearing and ball-play – for none of which, I may say, do the older hagiologies (for such is the sum of our literature) offer any authority. In troth the Oireachtas (Dinneen says the word means 'a synod') is a terrible exhibition of foreignism. Nay, worse. I know of no civilisation to which anything so self-conscious could be indigenous. Why go to the trouble of proving that you are Irish? Who has questioned this notorious fact? If, after all, you are not Irish, who is?

Here is an amusing bit I read in the paper the other day:

> Oireachtas Festival – Leading Irish composers, like Eamon O Gallachobhair, Capt. Michael Bowles and Redmond Friel, from Derry, have composed special works for the musical events of the festival . . .

Who, pray, are your men? We are given three clues –
(a) They are 'leading Irish composers';
(b) they are from Derry;
(c) they are 'like' Eamon O Gallachobhair, Capt. Michael Bowles and Redmond Friel.

Somebody pointed out recently that Sibelius was like Tchaikowsky. Just what is this quality of being 'like' somebody else? Does it connote imitation? A similarity of intuition? A slavish re-statement of things better said by the master? Or is this likeness physical, facial? I know a man who is like Bach, but he is a mutton factor and knows nothing of the well-tempered klavier. The three musical simulacra mentioned have done creditable work as musicians and I think it is a shame that their compositions will not be heard merely because there are more insistent candidates who resemble them. I do not hold it against these unnamed parties that they are from Derry but how come that they are *all* from there? Is there something in the Londonderry air . . . . that breeds leading Irish composers? Hmmmmm.

Here is another bit I read only yesterday – and I am translating literally, mind you:

Such literature and music as is not rooted in tradition and in the music of the people, it is not life but death that is in store for it . . .

This statement is reported as having been made at the official opening of the Oireachtas. Do I have to say that I dissent from it? I find as follows

(a) While literature may be rooted in tradition, it cannot be rooted in the music of the people.

(b) It is premature to be exclusive about the 'rooting' of literature, or the fate thereof, inasmuch as we have no literature (worth talking about – and in this country we require very slender pretexts for talk).

(c) The veneration of folk 'culture' norms, whether of story or song, as repositories of national treasure is ludicrous; inasmuch, of course, as they are international and universal, Indian, Icelandic and Kerry peasants will bore you with identical 'stories'.

(d) If nothing can live unless 'rooted in tradition', how come that the works comprising that tradition exist at all? Surely somebody has to begin . . . . somewhere?

I am not too sure about you Irish. Fair enough if you *like* step-dancing, competitions in 'story-telling' and shrill aberrations on the bag-pipes. My trouble is that I don't believe it. My observation tells me that most of you prefer horse-racing, coursing (aye, even cursing), poker, coorting, and the consumption of wines, beers and spirits on premises duly licensed therefor. Could you not have that sort of an Oireachtas? With me as President?

*Not in this case the machinery of government, but a great cultural festival of things Hibernian.

xii

We speak commonly of disease, dissolution and death as though these routines were set apart from the illusory business

of living (I nearly said 'loving'!) – as though they were symp-
tomatic of upheavals not part of the natural order, as though
they were the epiphenomenal accidents of incalculable metaphysical events, not allowed for in the original human
blue-prints for the universe. This casual attitude, arising partly
from a dialectical need, partly from the sense of dichotomy, of
conflict, which, deny it as we may, is endemic to the species,
need not be too harshly deprecated. Truth we know to be
unobtainable; many of us are not too sure of the 'existence' of
a 'reality' which could give it its most imposing dimension –
and so, in the pyrrhic encounter with *ennui*, we amuse ourselves by reading the apprehensible 'world' only in terms of
duality. (I trust I make myself clear.) We endlessly dramatise
what we are pleased to call 'life'. And, in point of fact, the element of theatre is there, there *is* a . . . struggle, there *is* . . . a
– given a *great* man, of course – there *is* a tragedy: above all,
there is dramatic irony. For 'unknown' to the spectator (Kant
has dealt rather fully with the illusory nature of physical 'cog-
nizances'), what is life but decay, what is existence if it be not
an unduly complex process of decomposition? What is life but
. . . . disease?

When this malady (call it the *morbus vivendi*) tends to reach
its climax, it is interesting to observe that the patient's consciousness of suffering . . . decreases: not only is his uneasy
'prescience' (or anticipation of disaster) extinguished, but yields
place to a gay anticipation of the world, an elation, an *élan*, an
ecstasy that is related inversely to the expectation of life. It is a
generalised *spes phthysica*.

In this rather large clinic which one may call 'the world', I
would with respect draw attention to the condition of the body
politic. For surely there you have these symptoms in evidence, as
perceptible and unambiguous as a fireworks display. I refer, of
course, to that international opium spree – post-war planning.
What a show the post-war world will be, what a gay gay party!

Now turn for a moment from that large-scale canvas, a masterpiece which belongs to no age, no race, no time and

contemplate one quaint and parochial reaction to this *inquié-tude du siècle* of the outer world. I am now speaking, as readers will be quick to recognise, of the . . . . . Irish Tourist Board, not so much as a Board but as a . . . . policy. The Boarders (I'm not sure that that is quite the term – your English language is so complicated) appear to think that after this war, when the demolition of the world shall have been finally accomplished, everyone – esquimeau, china-boy, new zealander, mexican, viennese – is going to be pretty sick and tired of his own place. Actually you can't escape this sickness by moving house but the Boarders seem to think that *everybody* – excepting possibly the emigrant Irish, who know a thing or two – will deem it a proper thing to come to your Eire, in order to reside here for months. This contingency (not to say this contingent) is to be provided for by providing a register of hotels and by taking steps to see that the town of Tramore is not water-logged. In no time, it appears, you will all be very rich, like the Swiss.

But stay, I beg ye! Is money everything? What of native culture? Assuming your visitors arrive (and that you are not put to the humiliation of having to return the bottle of brown sherry to the grocer), what will be the effect of this inundation of foreignism? Will they not disseminate anti-Gaelic ideas, saturate your people with a contempt for your immensely native network of censorships? Is it proposed to serve drink to these dagoes? Build . . . . dance-halls for them? Are you – surely not? – going to cater for their wretched foreign games? Obsolesce the philosophies so intimately connected with your D.J.s? It seems incredible, this ascetic, crimeless island Sparta, dedicated in a special way to learning and religion, it seems incredible that it should be metamorphosed into a mere . . . . . pleasure resort!

(No, no, I still can't connect the two . . . . . . Ireland . . . . . . and . . . . . . pleasure!)

xiii

Christmas again approaches. What is your parental attitude to the Santa Claus business? In some households, alas, even tiny tots cynically assure each other that 'it is only daddy.' I perceived many years ago the only way to combat this attitude. The child is terribly logical and will not tolerate two benevolent paternalisms. Tell your child of this other sky-borne daddy and the small philosopher will instantly suspect you of lying. With my own children I managed the thing in rather a beautiful way. I taught them that there *is* a Santa Claus, but that they have no father!

7

In His Own Country

*In which Myles na gCopaleen selflessly continues
to address the island's sundry ills, be they caused
by bad literature, disease or an unjust legal
system. Though Ireland may currently ignore his
homiletics, warning is given that the day may
not be far when a sorrowing nation will pay due
homage to a great prophet who fought for his
people, and for the world. His disciples Keats
and Chapman continue to struggle on the hard
edge of existence. Perhaps, as the foreign war
draws to a close, the whole country should go off
on holiday: Japan is recommended.*

i

On behalf of my constituents (the human race) whom I have had the honour of representing for so long on the Governing Body of the University of Life, I wish to express the regret we all feel that this should, at last, be 1945. It is, of course, nobody's fault – *all are absolved without qualification*. Indeed, one might pause to pay a well-deserved tribute to those thoughtful people who have been in recent years endeavouring to interfere, through the medium of high explosives, with the 'normal' movement of the heavenly bodies and thus disrupt the mechanism that conditions the mystical arcanum known as 'time'. For my own part, my conscience is crystal-clear. Warning after warning I gave of the approach of 1945 – both the day and the hour were predicted. No heed was taken and . . . . . now . . . . now it is too late. Your ship of life (the S. S. Marie Celeste) has departed on another voyage – destination unknown – captain drunk – the first mate a known murderer.

> *O navis! Referent in mare te novi*
> *Fluctus. O! Quid agis?**

*From Horace's *Odes* (1.XIV, 1-2): O ship! Modern waves are sweeping you out to sea. O! What are you to do?

ii

A word of apology and explanation. I am terribly busy at present with my scheme for unifying the National Health Insurance

Society and for some days I will be unable to reply to correspon-
dence save that of the greatest import. I cannot, for instance, reply
to the innumerable letters I receive from people asking me to help
them in writing their plays; perhaps they will accept this – the only
– intimation, as it would be impossible to reply individually.

It does occur to me, however, that quite a large number of
these would-be dramatists would benefit considerably by a *general* reply in these columns; for this reason, that I perceive the
same simple fault in nearly every one of the manuscripts sub-
mitted for my consideration. I mean the *characters* are all wrong.
Either there are too many characters, too few characters, or
characters of an unsuitable type. Wherefore I have decided to
print, for the benefit of all persons writing plays for the Abbey,
a definitive *dramatis personae*; only by adhering to this will it be
possible to write a successful play. Here are the characters:

Michael Dommiky.
Bridget Dommiky, his wife.
Angela Dommiky, their daughter.
Carney O'Glawsheen, a young farmer.
Mrs Shoolagin, a widow.
Mary, her maid.
Thade Crawbells, a neighbour.
Bella Crawbells, his wife.
Christy, a travelling man.
Workmen, threshers, policemen, etc.

Simple when you go the right way about it, isn't it? The actual
names can be changed, of course (indeed they often have been)
but there before you is the essential guts of any decent play. If
you are one for frills and fancy work, it is permissible to intro-
duce, as optional supernumerary characters, 1 lovable old
canon, 1 romantic school-teacher (male or female), 1 film-
making unit bent on putting Ballynanownshuch on the map, 1
masher on the motor-bike, or 1 'stranger'. Further than that you
dare not go; anything more than that were folly.

If you reflect on this set of characters, you will soon realise that they are equally suitable for comedy or tragedy and will serve even for that odd presentation that is described on its own playbill as 'A Play'. If you reflect further, you will realise that there is not a whole lot of difference between comedy and tragedy and if you will be counselled by me, you will give no clue as to which game you are at. (After all, a comedy that is unamusing is a tragedy, ask any producer.)

The action of this play? Well, that is a matter largely for yourself – *but rigidly subject to the following provisos as to time and place*:

ACT I   –   Kitchen in Michael Dommiky's house.
ACT II   –   Same. Two hours later.
ACT III   –   Courthouse, Ballynanownshuck.

N.B. – The curtain will be lowered during Act I to denote the passing of four years.

That, I think, is all. I've practically written the play for you; it's only a question of filling in a few blanks, getting together a few bits of dialogue, etc. Do not let me down, though, by forgetting about the will, the old bottomless well in the farmyard, the letter that falls into the wrong hands, the old man, thought long-since dead, who reappears, etc., etc.

The characters, of course, remain my property and can be used only under licence. They must in no circumstances be committed to licentious or unIrish situations – absolutely nothing but decent rural land-hunger and murder will be countenanced.

Let me know when your play is on so as I can be sure to be out of town.

iii

I regret to inform the sovereign Irish People (1922) Ltd, that I am suffering from a severe cold. I would not dream of mentioning the matter only that it is my stern duty to record the following absolutely certain 'cures' suggested by 'friends'. (I am sorry but I must go on with this.)

1. Stop in bed man, there's nothing for a thing like that oney stop on bed. It'll be the same at the latter end, you'll stop in bed. Bed is the only man for a dose like that.
2. Do what I do, fight it on your feet. Ignore the damn thing. I seen meself, in the year nineteen and twenty seven, puttin' on the tail coat and off down to the Gresham for a hop, temperature a hundred point four. Know what I'm going to tell you? The following mornin' . . . . .
3. Look, there's oney wan way to shift a cold. Into a chemist and ask for a dose of quinneen laced with tincture of angustura. Begob I well remember . . . . .
4. My advice to you is to have a good mustard bath and then into bed with a lemon drink, very hot. (Would bananas not help, I can't avoid asking.)
5. Hot milk me good man, you can't whack it.
6. Four aspireens goin' to bed with a little drop of port wine.
7. Maybe you think I'm ould-fashioned, but anny time *I've* a cold, I get an ould sock and (gestures are made) four times around the neck as tight as you can wind it . . . . .

A bad cold is – well – bad, but how about having a black eye. 'What happened your eye?'

iv

An Encounter

I said a good thing to an old cabby the other night. In a hurry out to Cabinteely to buy some carpet slippers for the granda, I hailed this Jem stuffed up somnolent on the box. After working on him for some time, managed to restore life, got in and off we went. Well it took us about an hour to get to Lansdowne Road. I opened the door, jumped out (difficult thing to do without opening the door) and shouted to this heavily moustached Ben Hur. Do you see this, says I, pointing to the good crombie overcoat. I do, says he, it's an overcoat. Good, says I, I was afraid you thought it was a coffin. NOW WILL YOU FOR THE SWEET LOVE AND HONOUR OF THE DEAD CHIEF . . . . USE THE SO-AND-SO WHIP! That's all very well to talk the old fool mumbled but you must know this is only a horse-drawn vehicle . . . . Indeed then and bejapers and I don't doubt you me good man says I for do you know what I'm going to tell you divil a human hand had hand act or part in the delineation of this rickshaw.

There was only one thing to do, of course. Unyoked the horse, got him over the railings into the Veterinary College and then in between the shafts with myself. Made Cabinteely in 40 minutes. No trouble to me, of course. I am, as you know, a hack!

V

I have written in many tongues, always in most extended form, in praise of poverty and humility: the one a condition, the other an attribute: both peculiarly Irish: the one attainable, capable of being put within the grasp of all by further and more patient research on the part of the Revenue Commissioners: the other a first-fruit of self-contemplation, and awareness of personal insignificance in the face of grandiose and permanent establishments to be seen on every side, e.g. the universe, the vast illimitable seas, the Most Honourable Order of the Knights of Columbanus, the law of diminishing returns, the way of an eagle, etc. Indeed, humility is so *necessary*, of a nature so all-pervading, so circumambient, that I often think that poverty is not a separate thing, only a component of humility. For add to poverty such other lofty attributes as abstinence from whiskey, Gaelic dancing, an unreadiness to be elected to the office of President of Ireland – and do they not together spell humility, this cicatricle of immortality?

Not having myself the honour to belong to the human race, I do not require myself to embrace the vocation of humility, inexorably as I must require others to take note of that virtue. I find, however, that the inter-identity of poverty and humility leads us to a strange crossroads. War, the savage imposition of the will of one upon another, is not possible among those who are humble of heart. The vast bulk of mankind is very poor and therefore very humble. Yet wars erupt . . . ? Wherefore these monstrous insanities?

I take leave to state that it will be necessary in the future for mankind to take vows of silence as well as vows of poverty and humility, because my researches lead me to the conclusion that wars may well be due to the use of speech. Even the very humble talk, a deplorable incompatability. It may sound ironical but this conclusion was borne in upon me the other morning at dinner (well – what are you staring at?) when I perceived a large heading as follows in our contemporary, the *Irish Times*:

HUMANITY IN PERIL IF TALKS FAIL

One finds that so amusing that it is almost impossible to resist inventing equally significant variants – Humanities In Peril If Talk Fails, Hugh Manity In Tails If Pearl Talks, and so on. But accepting this discovery of humanity, pray where would humanity be if not in peril? The reader knows as well as the present writer that the answer to that question is not to be enunciated among adult persons. The thing is really too excellent for words, particularly the notions it implicitly evokes: that talk, for example, is not itself the symbol of failure, the *apology* for inaction, the chosen organ of deception, forfeiture, inadequacy – the pretence that 'talk' and 'fail' are not joined in most poisonous symbiosis to form a cancerous excrescence on the heart of man, the savagely ironical suggestion that between *humanity* and *peril* (synonyms) stands only the concept, smug, pathetic, dreary, of 'successful talk'!

Do I seem bitter? Perhaps – a little. But, reader – do not forget that I was at Westphalia, grey, sinister, but – alas for Europe – unheeded, in 1648. Do not forget that in 1815 I travelled to Vienna with the Bishop of Autun, do not forget that I, solitary, immaculate, was at Fairyhouse in 1916. Who am I? (Smiles, inscrutable, ageless, takes reader's tiny hand in his, bows low . . . .) That, Madame, I *may* not tell – but *you* may call me *The Wondering Jaw*. Madame, à demain!

vi

How good to know Carrie Tasz – I MEANT *caritas* but no matter – to let anger, unexpressed, decline and sicken in the bosom, to be – after insult – mild, loving, slightly dismayed!

A quaternion of moons ago the writer of these notes (quem deus I greatly fear vult perdere) chanced to read in this (present) publication a literary article purporting to have come from the pen (O swan of talent!) of Mr Patrick Kavanagh, himself the author of a timber treatise entitled, I think, 'The Green Fuel'. Comment I did not make, did not dare to make – for I deemed it an asperson on my persion (and I am the first to admit that through an error the eye is in the wrong place there). The article was about The Younger School of Irish Realists . . . .

Which – to digress – immediately reminds me of this question of censorship. Would it be a help to do it this way – lay a copy of each book published by a Younger Irish Realist on the table of each House of the Oireachtas: and if within twenty-one sitting days (O parliamentary cluck!) each such house shall not have passed a resolution annulling such book, the said book shall be deemed to have passed both Houses of the Oireachtas and shall, on being signed by the President, become law? The Royal Irish Academy of Writhers should consider this suggestion – it would enable unsuccessful authors to have their work published as Government White Papers and give the immoral behaviour of apocryphal peasants a certain legal standing.

But here then is the passage that angered me so justly, compelled me to refrain from comment until the tide of wrath had ebbed:

'Frank O'Connor, writing once on Irish literature*, was only able to mention three writers. I do not think I could add to that number . . . .'

I make no remark on the location of the word 'only' in that context. I content myself with the assumption that the three writers concerned are Messrs S. O'Faolain, F. O'Connor and P. Kavanagh. And quite right! But . . . . would it have hurt so much to make it . . . . four? (Readers will note my almost unearthly calm in such a situation as this. Do I rant? Am I ravin'? (Nevermore!))

I have had, it is true, my day; I have known fame, have tasted the buttered suites of notoriety, have walked (when I was not carried) in the gilded palaces of prince and suzerain, have participated in the majesty of Kings, dined with brooched potent têtes of the orient. And now, forsooth, my lot is to be sackcloth and hashish. So be it! I remember the words of the preacher and I murmur to myself: 'There came one who knew not Joseph . . .' Protest I do not care to make, for pride is a very personal possession which must wither and rot when the ailments of the soul, the rusting mechanism of the psyche, the festering sores of the wounded heart are exposed or capitalised in any appeal for . . . . alms! Odi, odi, Prof. Annum Voelgus! For myself, as I say, I care nothing. Nothing at all. But . . . hurt my friends, offer injury to their fair name or reputations and then, sirs, the fight is on! Doctor Yeats – is he then forgotten? Joyce, whose little handbook on Dublin and its environs has brought so much sunshine into the lives of so many in so short a space, are ye also unmindful of his work for . . . . what did you call it? . . . . Irish literature? Dr D'Alton, whose six-volume history is still so fine a delight? John Mitchel himself – is his 'Ballad of Reading Gaol' become a despised bagatelle with the children of this age? Ah, bitter, bitter reward for many a tragic tomb!

*Actually, in 1944 in the English magazine, *Horizon*.

vii

The public will be heartened to learn that they will shortly be afforded an opportunity of paying tribute, not as heretofore in the boudoir of the inner heart, but openly – by acclamation, respectful obeisance and even overt monetary offering – to a distinguished soldier, stetsman (state) and . . . . presence who has for so long been preserving decency and order from this rostrum for sole long. I am at the moment engaged in fixing up the details with Hernon*. It is true that we have not yet quite come to terms – negotiations are necessarily long and, of course, protracted – but I expect to be able to make an important announcement shortly over the Flensburg Radio. You see, I am arranging to lie in state in the City Hall for three days. The Government of the Irish Republic is kindly providing a guard of honour and the catafalque will bear the flags of the United Nations. Watch this *spes* for further details.

*P J Hernon, in 1945 Dublin City Manager and Town Clerk.

viii

Chapman, having once spent the entirety of the morning examining himself in a mirror, mentioned to Keats that he was contemplating going on the stage. He had felt for some time, he said, that the stage was his vocation and was convinced that the inner intensity of his art would alone enable him to bring great aesthetic experience to mankind and also to win such as of fortune or fame was the portion of the great actor. During his earlier studies he would require from Keats the contents of the latter's purse. The security, he felt sure, was ample. Indeed, in addition to his endowments of genius (not then perhaps readily perceptible to the eye) he had other more palpable graces such as any actor might well envy. 'What?' Keats asked.

'Well . . . my looks,' Chapman said defiantly. 'You have prob-

161

ably yourself noticed that my face is mobile, full of character, and mysteriously attractive. Then my hair –' he inclined his blond head so abruptly that Keats had to jump up from his chair – 'pray notice not only the lovely hue, but feel how exquisitely fine in texture it is!'

'I hope it keeps fine for you,' Keats said, walking over some potato peelings into the kitchen.

ix

Yesterday in the District Court Feodor Mjizczoklzlav, with an address in Patrick Street, was charged with the illegal possession of two tons of tea, 8,145 bicycle tyres, a quantity of malt extract and two dozen razor blades.

A detective sergeant stated that at 4 p.m. on the morning of the 4th instant he proceeded to certain converted stabling premises at the rear of Patrick Street. Failing to gain admittance through the door, he entered through a skylight. On the premises he found the defendant and his wife. The defendant was making tea. The commodities mentioned in the charge were in a back room and covered with sacks. Asked to account for them, the defendant said they were the property of a man called 'Fennell' from Belfast. He did not know the present where-abouts of Fennell. He had agreed to caretake the articles and await instructions. He was then charged and cautioned. He said 'that will be all right' but made no further statement.

Defendant, speaking from the dock, stated he wished to challenge the accuracy of the police officer's statement. It was not a fair or complete statement of what happened.

Justice   – In what respect is it wrong?

Defendant   – I am sure the Sergeant can explain that. (To Sergeant:) After you entered my rooms did I make a savage assault on you, tearing the right sleeve of your uniform and causing discolouration over your left eye?

Sergeant   – You did not.

Defendant – Then where did you get that mark over your eye?

Sergeant – I slipped on the roof when I was getting in.

Defendant – Did I at any time strike you?

Sergeant – At one stage you tripped over something on the floor and accidentally gave me a shove.

Defendant – You admit I shoved you?

Sergeant – Yes.

Defendant, addressing the Court, asked that the Sergeant's replies to his questions should be carefully noted. He felt sure that the want of a positive element in these replies arose from the Sergeant's lofty concept of duty and the regard, not to say affection, in which he held all persons, no matter how depraved in criminal vice, who chanced to come into his custody in the course of duty. He (defendant) must solemnly assure the Court that he had brutally assaulted the Sergeant. The 'shove' referred to was a violent assault at the officer's stomach. He (defendant) had also used foul language and if he did not actively resist arrest (which he denied he did not) it was because of unworthy fears of the immediate physical measures which would have to be taken to correct so deplorable an attitude. As regards the tea, tyres and blades, he declared that in addition to having harboured these essential stuffs in open and profligate defiance of the laws and regulations promulgated by the Government for the safeguarding of the public, particularly the poor, the offence was more serious than that: the goods were uncustomed and had in fact been stolen from reputable traders. Continuing, defendant said that he could attribute his inexplicable and beastly behaviour to a brute lust for comfort and wealth, the sort of affluence that is all the sweeter for being secured at the expense of the less fortunate. He did not wish to distress the Court by a more particular description of his own base nature. He contented himself by asking for the heaviest penalties imaginable.

The *Chief State Solicitor* said that his instructions did not permit him to press for the death penalty.

Defendant suggested a short adjournment to enable the Solicitor to confer with his principals.

The *Justice* said the Court was one of summary jurisdiction; his own duty was to administer the law as he found it. He therefore sentenced the defendant to six months imprisonment.

Defendant – Without hard labour? If there is no hard labour I will appeal. This is a travesty of justice.

Defendant was led below, protesting loudly.

X

And now – a toast! 'The Ladies! God bless their little hearts!' (Icy silence.) Ah! Have I perhaps said the wrong thing? In the simple, homely things, in the eternal, unchangeable things, in the wholesome joists (sorry, joys) of home life do the young women of today no longer take pleasure? These and a host of kindred ideas no whit less pleasant suffused the head of the writer of these notes on reading a recent report which . . . em . . . which purported to appear under the heading IRISH AUTHORESSES' OPPORTUNITIES. How many times must I ask editors and all who are in high station to observe a little more circumspection: straight spection can be carried too far – like My Excellency on Saturday nights. (It's at No. 12 I live, *not* 22: voluntary workers pl. note.) How often must I point out that stories of sensational and ugly happenings, murder, divorce, bankruptcy, marriage, etc., are highly repugnant to the spirit and letter of our Constitution, subversive of public morality, contrary to holy charity and offensive in a special way to the metropolitan canons of good taste and divers other chapters under my tutelage. Duchesses I have heard of (nay! have married . . . . . . mostly, be it admitted, to dukes); the buttress and the harness I know, the sombre cypress I find it in my heart to reverence. But authoresses! ('What is an authoress, Mr McBride?' 'Milord, an authoress is . . . .') Authoresses? Neagh, *Irish* authoresses? What . . . what dread latterday unChristian tomfoolery is this? Their opportunities – ? Just heavens, what may *they* be? Have they, fur suit, opportunities denied to other Irishwomen, just as handsome, just as good? Has the Imperial Government, Merrion Street Upper, withdrawn from them the immemorial right to . . . . . to rock the cradle? Or how else, in what more fitting manner, with what ampler grace or distinction hope they to . . . rule the world? Egad, I know not: but let me, for the nonce, read from this document which has been put in evidence and attributed to the President of the Women Writers' Club:

'Having been saved from the war, the women writers of Eire had a unique opportunity before them . . . .'

Here, needless to say, we have the usual thing: an attack on myself. You see the insinuation. *I*, of course, *wasn't* saved from the war. I'm the one supposed to be across the other side all the time working for the other crowd, broadcasting in Gaelic to the Free Irish. And now, of course, I'm supposed to be dead, and the girls is going to write what they like because the magistral throne is vacated. Well, I'm *not*, and you can forget about that opportunity; the whole lot of you can take your scarlet finger-nails off my typewriter and get back into the scullery before I tell you. And I'm glad to see my old friend, Lynn Doyle*, takes the same view and says so in no uncertain terms at the same party, or so, at least, it's reported:

'Lynn Doyle urged women writers to keep to domestic affairs and ignore history, humour and warfare . . . .'

Aye, and literature when they're at it, as God intended. But the Doctor added a very cryptic remark. I didn't quite get it:

'The future of the novel must be the future of women, he added.'

What – on the shelf? (Never read anything written by a woman meself barring those notes pinned to the dressing table: 'Gone to Belfast with Basil. Your dinner is in the oven. Cad and womanbeater!') At the same party another lady said another lady's book was scholarly, entertaining, diverting and informative, and combined many qualities which were rare in present-day writing. Hmmmmm. I'll say this. Some of the things that are rare today there's a very good reason for their rarity. I see Austin Clarke† was there too. What's the idea of never inviting me to these things? I combined a good few qualities meself in me day.

*Leslie A Montgomery (1873-1963), humorous Irish writer and lecturer, used the pen-name Lynn C Doyle ('linseed oil').
†Austin Clarke (1896-1974): eminent Dublin critic, broadcaster, poet and wearer of corduroy trousers.

xi

Civis Romanus *homme*. I am of course a visitor here (just when does a visitor become an inhabitant? The wife's 'brother' has been on a 'visit' in my house since 1924) but that is not to say that I am destitute of posed war plans for the land of May had option I beg pardon the land of my adoption. Readers will be aware of the constitutional position. We are in the Empire but not Ovid. Distinguished British statesmen resident in Co. Belfast have seen fit to make discourteous references to your republic, even suggesting that it would be no harm if you packed up and clear doubt! I . . . . . I wonder would Mister Churchill really like it that way? Take a look at Ireland:

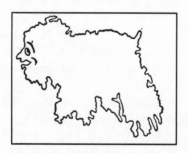

Does it look to you like a timorous, depressed, decadent country? A land afraid of the future? A realm with no prospects?

In reality it looks jaunty and gallant, very much as if it were going to go places. Suppose . . . . . suppose I were to tell you that I have devised a system of . . . . . land migration, a system based on liquefaction and pumping such as would enable the sovereign republican government of your Ireland to . . . . . literally to run the country, have it go and come as they please? Suppose you were, early one morning, to leave the so-called Empire in the most devastatingly literal sense, simply disappear bag and baggage? Wouldn't the British be just a little bit sorry? Know for the first time what you so patiently put up with from the Atlantic Ocean? And where to go? Well, *there* is one idea. Set up house in the middle of the mild blue Mediterranean, become hot Latin persons.

Observe, reader, the bare forsaken aspect of England and Scotland on that map. Do they want it that way? Do they *really* want to traverse the Bay of Biscay and squeeze in through the tortuous portals of Gibraltar just to have a steak in Dublin? Do they seek a situation wherein a visit to Ireland even for the purpose of collecting debts involves an expensive ocean voyage? I doubt it very much. And let me add that if your somewhat severe governors think that there is much to be said against the South of France as a latitude unsuitable for your Ireland, why –

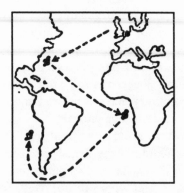

– there are other places. What's wrong with being anchored off New York harbour? Would not that substantially reduce the expenses of emigration? *And* if that ultimately bores, there are, as I have shown on my map, other places. (And still others – I understand the climate is very temperate around Japan?)

Certain is this much: you are the worst in the world because you're here; and if you go away you'll be the worst in the world.

xii

Mr Myles na gCopaleen has left town (i.e. Moscow) for two weeks and his daily discourses must be discontinued for that period. Any inconvenience to readers is regretted.

8

Into Infinity

In which Myles na gCopaleen takes his leave, shattered by mankind's betrayals during a short absence on spiritual matters. If the world wishes to make its decisions alone, so be it, but when his own private agonies are travestied in the public prints as well, it is time to go. His suffering body is easily discarded, and now his spurned spirit must also make its exit, a broken corpse astride a speeding bicycle. To comfort the few good souls who may still follow his words he leaves behind him a cruse of oil: Cruiskeen Lawn. It will continue to write itself after he has gone. Myles na gCopaleen's long war is over, and his Golden Hours have passed into history for ever.

i

W.E.L.L.!

I hope everybody is satisfied. I hope all are now *completely* happy.

Readers will join me in offering My Excellency heartfelt condolences on the recent occurrences. Consider what happened. My back is turned for fourteen brief days. (Believe me, it was essential: readers who have the honour to be 'human' (i.e., poor) and who find it necessary to have their clothes turned occasionally will readily understand about my back.) During my absence, during the short disinhabitation of the rostrum whereon resides my absolute authority, during my most voluntary immurement within Melleray*, events base and felonious, terrible in their enchargement with vanity and folly, were suffered to occur. The first treasonable eruption took place at St. Souci, County Potsdam, where a number of United Statesmen, meeting secretly in the apartments of Friedrich le Grocer, saw fit to issue a 'Declaration' purporting to effect the destiny of the earth! Mark well the devastating presumption of those abandoned men. At a central point on the continent of Europe they convene a conference for the purpose of promulgating a plan for the resettlement *for all time* of European affairs. How many European nations, artificers and custodians of true culture, were represented at that conference? It is laughable, but the answer is *not one*! They were not present – not even in the dock! Indeed rumour was rife *that they were all dead* and that this conference was in reality concerned with taking out letters of administration, the deceased parties having died intestate! *And*, apparently, when you die intestate there, your entire estate goes, as a matter of etiquette, to M. Stalin. W-e-l-l! It is scarcely necessary for *me* to say that the whole transaction is destitute of legality, all the documents pertinent thereto devoid of the requisite initials M. na gC. The men concerned are peace criminals and will be dealt with in time according to my laws.

What shall I say of the atomic grenade lately perfected in America and subsequently exported to Japan, duty free? It is an astounding achievement, not so much in physics as in the more familiar sphere of human folly. I am aware that for humans there has been a long-standing arrangement whereby they can be absolutely sure of one thing, each for himself, i.e. death. There is no case on record of the pledge given to man that he will die having been broken. Yet scientists and governments are very worried about the possibility that people may not die, or may not expire in sufficiently gigantic numbers, and, *in order to make sure*, have devoted much thought and treasure to research on this subject. The most efficient device yet evolved appears to be this 'atomic bomb'. I do not find that the quest for it is an adult performance.

Why should this outsize barbarity be visited on the Japanese? It cannot be because Japan was at war with America, since human rights remain intact even in war and the admirable Red Cross Society exists to see that these rights are meticulously respected. No, it must be because the Japanese are considered unpleasant folk; few of them are Knights of Columbanus, Elks or Rotarians, they are not afraid of death, they respect authority and live frugally. And they have manners. Contrast the affront offered to my person by the Potsdam occurrence with this urbane and respectful reference to me in a recent report on His Excellency Emperor Hirohito:

'Returning to Japan, he broke with tradition by marrying a girl with whom he was in love. Of his six children, five live in the Palace . . .'

Could anything be more delicate? Not a hint of my abode, my

tasks, my absorbing interest in man, my anxiety that he shall not destroy himself utterly?

*Mount Melleray Abbey welcomed guests for teetotal retreats.

ii

Talking still of the abombic tomb – I *meant* atomic bomb but leave it, I am a neutron in such matters – readers will have noticed no doubt with distaste that news of the invention evoked the customary speculations as to its possible 'peace-time' uses: what was the first possibility mentioned by every moron, in unambiguous defiance of the rules of taste and behaviour so often here set forth? *A grave wonder as to whether the Queen Mary could be driven across the Atlantic on a minute quantity of the stuff.* Readers will sympathize with me in recalling that improvements in air travel are measured solely with reference to the consumption of meals. The construction of engines developing 100,000 horse-power is not in itself noteworthy. But if these engines, fitted to aircraft, enable certain apocryphal eccentrics to have breakfast in Dublin and lunch in New York, then these engines are wholly startling and admirable. Another school of wonder-mensuration insists on an oblique application of this norm of feeds. They complicate the comparison by introducing newspapers. They are not completely impressed by technical innovations which make possible merely the consumption of consecutive feeds in dissimilar hemispheres. But if solemnly assured that recent advances in aeronautics makes it possible that a newspaper printed on the previous night in New York *can be on a Dublin breakfast-table the next morning*, then they are astounded, they advise their wealthier friends to get rid of all railway shares, pointing out that in the future it will be 'all air'. (Funny, My Grace opines, that nobody admires the aeroplane because it enables people to have breakfast in Dublin and be either roasted alive or drowned in time for lunch.)

Some people are very despondent about the atomic invention. All the commentators agree that there is no remedy for this awful discovery. Yet My Excellency hastens to reassure humanity. There *is* a simple remedy. Get out expensive invitation cards, vast scientific conference in the earth's noblest city (Belfast?), banquets, lectures, debates on the release of atomic energy, conferring of decorations on distinguished physicists, pious avowals that science is the handmaid of humanity etc., etc. Let every big scientist be there, let the party go on for a fortnight, make sure a good time is had by all. Then, very quietly, very efficiently, shoot every one of the ghouls who knows even a little about the atom. Burn all the papers and books on the subject. Get back to decent plain bombing with blockbusters, incendiaries and blazing oil.

iii

Keats and Chapman, travelling in America, once took up residence, entirely by accident, in a prohibited area used by scientists for testing primitive atomic bombs. A number of tramps were in residence in derelict huts, and this led the two friends to imagine the place was a settlement rather than a very dangerous bomb range.

One night a species of atomic bomb was dropped in the area. The dread instrument produced a number of freak effects, the most noteworthy of which was to blow the backs off several humans, leaving them alive, conscious, and otherwise intact. Chapman arrived back from the nearest village to find Keats minus his entire back, lying face down on the wreckage of a bed and cursing loudly. His lungs, uninjured, could be seen, with other organs, functioning normally. Chapman hastily improvised a temporary back of cardboard, and gave the poet two grains to induce sleep.

Morning revealed another wonder. All the human backs blown off by the bomb were to be seen piled in a heap in a nearby field. Keats, still cursing loudly and vowing vengeance on the bombers, insisted on stumbling in among the bleeding backs, surveying them carefully. Chapman took exception to the poet's language.

'You mustn't talk like that,' he remonstrated. 'This is an outrage, but it is not for human agents to exact retribution. Vengeance is not for mortals. Please come away from this ghoulish repository of flesh . . . . .'

'I'm going to get my own back,' Keats said savagely, turning over nearby fleshes.

iv

Readers should be familiar with my theory – sorry, my statement – that man is merely an objective phenomenon, a private hallucination of my own, not so much my faithful subject as my priceless object, my personal anonymentity, my household inanimity. Yet this inert and homemade . . . . being, albeit incapable of initiating any meritorious action, can sometimes, by sole virtue of my approval, please ('me' understood). The immediate occasion of these delights, so rare, so evanescent, are by me recognised as 'accidents' (in the phenomenal, not the philosophical sense, of course). I take a simple example, if only for the reason that your agony in attempting to apprehend a difficult example would cause me so much sympathetic pain. Consider the arts, activities especially dear to me by reason of the fact that I have damn the thing else to do with my time. So-called works of art – a very small number of them needless to say – have succeeded in pleasing me.

Let no man, intoxicated by foolish and block-headed inanity, imagine that such artistic successes reflect credit on the artists concerned or that the 'concern' of such operations plays any appreciable part in the réclame. (It's *not* the same thing – read it over again.) No conscious effort, no directed action of the 'artist' is of any value in the production of a work which may please me. How then to explain my recognition of certain efforts as being . . . worthy? Solely by a clear understanding of the fact that beauty is all my eye – I *am* sorry – that beauty is all *in* my eye! (Hmmm.) In *this* world, this universe, this system, man's 'greatness' is measured in direct ratio to his imitative, reflective, monkey-like faculties. Man is the mirror I delight in holding up to the magnificence of nature (Ah, poor Willie Wordsworth!), and if I haven't broken him long ago, it is only because of the seven years' bad luck. To man, the great planner, why, I am sure, the whole modality of events must seem like a chapter of accidents – never does he appear to appreciate that this is because the project has been initiated, sanctioned and put in hands . . . . elsewhere. Never is this innocent the agent he pretends to be; rather is he the material as fully set out in the invoice. He has never seen the invoice, and is consequently amazed when, having set out to cycle into town for five cigarettes he finds himself at the end of the day in Donegal Jail with a friend purporting to be an officer in a foreign airforce 'home' 'on leave'. (*Now* do you see what I'm getting at? I arranged the whole thing (years ago)!)

V

Have you heard the *latest*? I know we all know the way the crowd below in Belfast are never happy till they pack up their hard hats and move down here for good an' all, we all know the way they try to copy everything we do, we all know the way nothing would do them only have a small Dáil with clever statesmen, just like yeerselves, above in Stormont – but who'd ever have thought that we'd live to see *that* position reversed? Well, we have! Did you read there a little while ago about the exhibition the Cork Hill brigade made of themselves? Apparently what they're after now is turn the City Haul into a regular Orange Lodge and have drums, processions and demon-

strations just like our more civilized brethren in the Royal Black
Watch Commonwealth of Co. Portadown!

Well, of course, everyone knows my opinion about that sort
of thing – first of all it's going to embarrass the decent wee
Northernmen, because it never occurs to *them* that it's smart or
fashionable to be Northern – *they're* just *born* that way.
Secondly, if the Dublin Corporation are doing this in a wild
effort to make themselves more ridiculous, I think they're
wasting their time; *everyone* is delighted with them and thinks
they couldn't *possibly* be funnier than they are. Thirdly, the
thing is impracticable, particularly the way they're tackling it –
here's the newspaper report:

'Councillor —— suggested, on the grounds of expense, that
on ceremonial occasions sashes bearing the city arms should be
substituted for the robes . . .'

Sashes!! (I thought first he might have meant ordinary up-
and-down timber sashes, with exquisite little stained glass panels
let into the skeleton and fixed in the usual lead cames and possibly illuminated be torches embedded in the alderman's
waistcoats and I thought begob the idea isn't half bad, give the
I.T.B.* something to go to town on: 'Come to Dublin for the
Lord Mayor's Magic Lantern Procession!' Then I realised, of
course, I must be wrong because as sure as fate you'd have an
outcry from the metal window people on the advertising end of
it – you *know*!)

Sashes? Well, I know the robes look a bit quare, but everyone
knows what they are and the chislers can shout 'Hey, you in the
red flannel petticoats!' and the thing is . . . . entertainment in the
way God intended. But sashes! Would they wear them tied
around their middles and fastened at the front with a bit of an
oul' pussycat bow, I wonder? And would there be a fancy design
on the back? Or just their own arms tied behind, the City Arms?
That would be dignified all right, the black monkey-jacket and
sthriped throusers – cuffed to the knee – and then wrapped
around the 'waist' the old flag of Erin, three harps on a blue
field, the harps of Milesius? Or the other act, as practised across

the border – the blue serge suit, the brown boots, the stiff 2"
collar, the black bowler and . . . . neatly dhraped from shoulder
to waist-line the beautiful pink satin sash 2 yards @ 6d. a yard
in Camden Street?

Apparently they had another bright idea (I suppose the
Corporation is one way of helping fellows to keep their minds
off their work) which was this:

'The Committee which drafted the Standing Orders had suggested that robes should be provided for the members.
Eventually it was decided to adopt some form of symbol . . .'

What sort of symbol? Or do they mean cymbal? Now *there*
would be something to warm the cockles of your heart, the big
mór-shiubhal† coming down Dame Street headed be the Lord
Mayor playing the tambourine for dear life and behind the
merry clamour of triangle, kettle-drum and all the other small-
arms of the percussion family!

Tell you what would be as good a symbol as any – let each
man wear a large . . . corporation! (I suppose *now* I've said the
wrong thing . . . again.)

*Irish Tourist Board.
†Procession.

vi

Last week I went down to Wexford because I happen to have
some apple trees planted there, and I hold – doggedly – that I
am perfectly entitled to inspect them. Very well. So far so good.
I take a walk along the strand at Rosslare – what I am pleased to
call the *murrough nostrum*. I decide to swim. Afterwards I go
back to my hotel and consume my simple but nourishing repast
of hake and cider. All very usual and ordinary, nobody could
pretend that I was trying to draw a tension to myself. Later I
leave by air – and please note I never use aeroplanes – for
England on a private mission. Noted most carefully be it that I
was minding my own business, an occupation which embraces

all mineral, human and vegetable activity on this globe. Again so far so good. *Now* what happens? Next day I open my paper. Here is what I see.

What spectators describe as a thunderbolt fell into the sea off the Wexford coast. They saw a ball of blue fire rushing vertically into the sea, accompanied by a loud and hissing noise . . . Trees were blasted and cattle and horses bolted in terror . . .

Could impertinence and offensiveness go further? I am a 'ball', I am 'blue', and I 'hiss'! (!!). How did these sinful men describe my arrival in Britain? Read this:

A cyclone, described as "like an aeroplane diving with its engines full out" left a trail of devastation in the Hampshire village of Tichfield yesterday . . . Tiles were blown about like snowflakes . . . .

Is it not the limit?

vii

I am aware that a number of readers are life-long abstainers from intoxicants because they are persuaded that I disapprove of drink and that they, consequently, cannot drink without incurring my grave displeasure. This is not quite the fact. I myself have been known to drink, usually in Muddereashion (near Swanlinbar), holding, as I do, that the saturation of the viscera with poisonous fluids affords opportunity for the cultivation of pain, nausea and the fear of death as an invaluable spiritual therapy. Drink I hold to be praiseworthy also because it is responsible for the largest joke ever propagated, viz., that abstinence from alcohol (involving bounding health, clear vision, flawless nerves and financial prosperity) is a mortification, a hardship to be borne only by mystics – as against indulgence in alcohol (involving the decay of the organs, wrecked homes, murder, theft, paralysis and sudden death).

viii

I will issue no further warnings but will simply reserve to myself the absolute right to take such action as I may in my absolute discretion (or even secretion) think fit relative to the immediate promulgation of a mandatory nine-point directive purporting to govern the activities of certain journals appearing in the Irish Frieze State. Some time ago, accompanied by my aides, I chanced all in the evening down Dublin town to stroll. (Remember the time I was brought home from my 'recital', aided by my accompanists?) We had dined – wisely, but not too well – and the delicate plumes of cigar-smoke which convoyed our elegant dinner-jacketed figures homewards bespoke an urbanity, an authority, which unfailingly set us down as men-about-turn. One of us (as I must insist on calling myself) wanted a glass of milk and as, at that moment, we had arrived at a public house, it would, I hold, have been merest affectation not to enter. This we did without delay, mine most churlish host having failed to appear to the imperative summons we did not think unfit to address to him. Entering, one found himself alone; from the landlord – not a sign! One keenly felt the indignity of one's position but could not of one's original demands abate one jot. Milk one must have and immediately. No milk was observed but before searching for it, I did not hesitate to point out to myself that we could not afford ourselves the luxury of ignoring the common courtesies just because the innkeeper did. Anything we might find it necessary to take, I insisted, would have to be paid for, directed into the cache (register), in solid ringing florins of recognised colour and texture. Then it was that we remembered that we were attired en grandtenue de soir – nothing in the pockets for fear of spoiling our figures. There was then nothing forehead but to obtain – temporarily to borrow – some coins. Possibly there would be some of these plebeian medals in the safe? Judge of our surprise to find that the tavern-keeper, in an agony of suspicion and misanthropy, had locked the machine!!! Baffled, we decided not to let the whole evening thus be ruined and so insisted on instituting a search for the milk – a vain and fruitless search as it turned out. (Nor did a search for fruit prove any whit more milkful, alas!)

Dismayed, we sat down to think. I was parched with the thirst. These bottles, we asked myself, in them could there possibly be milk? Investigation of a bottle marked 'Genuine Old French Brandy' proved that this was not milk and in an effort to extinguish the consequent laceration in one's throat, we found it necessary to smoke some cheap cigars which lay on the counter. To say that we smoked them over a sloe fire and inhaled the aroma is nothing but the truth. It was unpalatable. By now, feeling very ill, we descended to the cellars where we found some policemen carousing in an unseemly way; entering into the spirit of the thing, we asked them to lend us a fiver for a taxi home, which they promptly did. We have ever since been on a bed of pain and were twice operated on as a result of this terrible evening. Judge then of our surprise and disgust on coming too (stet) to read in a diurnal newsletter this abject and vulgar distortion of the whole occurrence, under the heading THIEVES FAILED TO OPEN SAFE (!!!): 'Having failed to open the safe, they drank the best brandy and smoked the best cigars they could find, and stole £5 in coppers from the cellar.' ('from coppers in the cellar', obviously.)

Then it goes on to say, with monstrous effrontery: 'The police are investigating the occurrence . . . .'

Impertinence!

ix

I have written many words here in defence of all that is holy. There are not, of course, many things in this world properly to be ranked as holy, but instantly to be discerned as partaking of that estimable quality are chastity, poverty, and, em, endemic slimness. Holiness, by the way, *is* to be confused with happiness. The happy are holy, the holy are happy. Indeed, Gen. Haley, revered American militarist, esteemed destructor of Hiroshima, is, I understand, hoppy – injured his ankle when a youth. Hunger also is a very fine thing – notwithstanding the hotheads who occasionally strike against it. I have myself never had the honour to experience it for a rather simple reason – *I have no body*! Into the brackets for a moment – I'll make it worth your while! – and I'll tell you why. (Readers file dutifully into brackets, are surprised and pleased to find attendant at threshold serving small ones. (Are slightly disquieted to find they are expected to enter further interior brackets. (Master resumes peroration. (I'll tell you about me body. (I had one up to 1939 – *but never again*! It's about the greatest mugs' game out. I sold it in June, 1939, refused flatly the usual cajoling to trade it in for a new one, and I don't know meself since I got rid of it. The relief! The sense of . . . freedom, safety, absence of worry!

They say that the steam locomotive is about 8% efficient. I would rank the human body as about 2% if there was any way of rationalising the efficiency of a machine so complicated. The ticker, for instance, has leaky valves. If it stops once, the whole job is useless, no matter how sound the liver or lungs, you can throw the whole thing away. It hasn't even a scrap or remainder value. Put say two bottles of whiskey into the stomach and what happens? Hell to pay, the entire mechanism disorganised, eternal friendship pledged to strangers, gold watch presented to tram conductor and lethal capacity of Canal Co.'s locks surveyed following morning. Add to that the risk, so permanently run by persons with bodies, of being arrested by policemen! Or . . . or the danger of leaving it behind in a bus! Imagine the humiliation of ringing up C.I.E.* the next morning. 'I left my body in the last bus to Terenure last night.' 'What size sir?' 'O, it was fairly old, medium size, grey hair and paunch, waistcoat plastered with ash. It was fairly drunk.' 'No sir, it hasn't come in yet.' 'Well if it comes in during the day, would you have it left in the Dolphin. I'm going to Cork this week but I'll collect it when I get back and pay any expenses.' Or imagine, not having a gold watch, your inebriated attempts to present it to a conductor. 'Look, is this any use to you? You're welcome to it.' 'No sir, thanks very much but I have one.' 'Nonsense man, go on, take it.' 'I couldn't sir, I couldn't manage two.' 'But look, if you don't take it, I'm going to throw it away.' 'O very well.' Then a huff – and the exaggerated gesture of trying to stuff it into a street refuse-can. Bah! (Looks at readers who are blue-faced owing to low oxygen content of atmosphere. (Do yez want to get out? Very well. Concludes brackets.))))))

*Córas Iompair Éireann, the Irish Transport System (whose device; known as 'the flying snail', adorned the nation's buses and rolling stock).

X

Well here we are! Seems strange, eh?

I suppose I might as well admit it (I will be found out anyway) – I've been in a home – *again*!

Phew.

Phewwwwww! . . .

I was in a home and, strange to say (voice quavers with last desperate note of courage) I may tell you that I am not . . . I am not in the least bit ashamed of meself . . . I've had me troubles. Though truth to tell (begins to weep slightly) truth to tell and I don't believe I ever consciously told a man a lie, I . . . I got a great kick out of it. I know I'm no use, I've caused nothing but trouble in me time, I've received nothing . . . nothing but kindness from everybody. I only hope that wan day I'll be in position to repay. I . . . I hope and pray that everybody – ME ENEMIES INCLUDED – will . . . will participate in . . . . in . . . . (*here voice trails off in descriptions of country mansions peopled with servants and silverware*).

Why was I in a home, reader, you have the effrontery to ask?

Well, I could dissemble, could lie, could be evasive – even make the gigantic joke that *every man's life is his own*. (Monstrous gibe.) No, I am a secret drinker. Some of the secrets that I have drunk in me time would make you queerer than even me! *That's* saying something – as indeed the man said when he said 'Something'!

xi

Hallo there! Another Christmas begob. Another year gone, well well.

Well well.

I'll tell you this much. It's not younger we're gettin'.

Possibly we are getting older.

Another week of nineteen and forty-five and then we're into nineteen and forty-six. I'll tell you one thing about nineteen and forty-five. In no year in me life did I put in more hard sufferin'. I nearly went to the wall. The uncle was put through the loop and I had to stand in with four of the cousins, a tenner a skull. You might think that would make me down-hearted?

No doubt.

I think I got more of a kick out of nineteen and forty-five than I got out of any year bar wan. And that was nineteen and thirty-two, the year I fractured me back. Did I tell you about that?

You did not.

A lad let a pick-axe fall down on top of me from four storeys above in Mary's Abbey. I was on a bike, bent double pushin' against the wind. I run into a wall. Do you know why?

I do not know why.

After me back got the belt of the pick-axe, off with me for a scorch of a hundred yards at a battery of fifty miles an hour. Dead to you world, you understand, sittin' on the bike like a dead corpse, face as white as a sheet. Knocked out be the axe. Did you ever hear that sayin The Dead Ride Fast?

Yes. It is from Goethe. Die Toten reiten schnell.

I fly into the wall at a good fifty miles an hour. I got a sore crack on the head for meself. I was opened so wide the crowd thought the brain was hurt. The back was in two pieces, of course, broken in two be the axe the lad thrun down from the roof-top. The bicycle was made a *prawshick* of and there was a woman with a pram there that had a miraculous escape. And Me Nibs for dead on the path. What do you think of that?

Nothing.

Give me your hand. Feel me back here.

I will not.

Do you know what I have there? I have a cylinder made of silver jointed into me back with gold nails. They were for puttin' a silver plate into me head only the bone knit up again. I was in splints and plaster of paris for eight months, couldn't move hand, foot nor head. And I'll tell you this and it's as true as I'm here. I got one big kick out of it all. I spent nearly all that year in hospital and I don't think I ever enjoyed meself more. I was ordered onto the stout. Imagine Me Nibs lyin' back in bed scoffin' porter!

I can imagine.

And the year goin' out had its ups and downs too – I enjoyed every second of it. You heard me bike was pinched in March?

No.

Never seen sight nor trace of it since. Shook me up a bit. A thing like that is a sort of tonic. A man can do with a thing like that every three months. Makes you wake up and think. Shakes up the blood – the white corporals and all the rest of it. Like the other uncle that had fits when he was stoppin' with us. It was what they call An Object Lesson. Do you know what it done to us all, the uncle included?

What did it do to you?

It took us out of ourselves. And I got a great kick out of it because I gave that uncle a perfect cure.

What was it?

Two aspireens and a glass of port half an hour before retirin'. After two doctors had given the man up. That was in nineteen and thirty-five. Life is like a book. There's different chapters in it. There's something good in every chapter, but you have to read the whole book or you won't get the hang of the chapters. Do you folly me?

You mean you must die to comprehend life?

I often thought – do you know what it is – I often thought if I was to die tomorrow I'd get a bit of a kick out of it. It's the way I'm made. The way I look at it is this – it's *natural*. Do you twig? It's natural.

Certainly not this conversation.

I'm afraid I won't be seein' you over. I'm into Jervis Street Christmas Eve to get the toe opened. They do put on a great Christmas show there every year.

Happy Christmas.

Cheers now. And mind yerself!

Today
is Christmas Eve.
Some wretched readers may
take the view that today
at least they are entitled
to a holiday from my
discourses and that they
should, for once, be
spared the agony, humiliation,
shame and tears which contact
of humans with my mind
must ever mean.
Alas, I did not promise
such remission to any man
of
Wyman, Bourne (Monmouthshire).
The suffering must go on.

The Irish Times will not
be published tomorrow or the
day after. But in Thursday's
issue I will have three
discourses.
Order your coffin
in advance.

24th December 1945

·MEMENTO·
·MORI·
·SIC·
·TRANSIT· GLORIA·MUNDI·
· REQUIESCAT·
IN· PACE·

Acknowledgements

I thank the Brian O'Nolan estate for permission to reproduce his work here. I thank Senator David Norris for the indefinite loan of his uncle's scrapbook and hereby promise to return it at last. Hector McDonnell will never be thanked enough for his kindness in producing his fine drawings, but I thank him as much as possible anyway. My thanks are also due to the *Irish Times*, which had the sense and courage to publish 'Cruiskeen Lawn' in the first place, and to the Rev. Bertram Walsh, Peter Costello, Julie Moller, Anthony Cronin, Bernard McGinley, Tess Hurson, Simon Campbell, Rory Campbell, Paul Quarrie, Martin Rynja, Stephen Curran, Karen Wadman and the late John Ryan for help and a variety of intelligent suggestions. I also thank Daniel, Conor, the entire extended Wyse Jackson family, and all at John Sandoe (Books) Ltd in Chelsea, for their forebearance in the face of quite unreasonable Mylesian provocation. My own contribution towards the preparation of this book is dedicated, with love, to my wife Ruth.

Sources

All selections are from 'Cruiskeen Lawn' by Myles na gCopaleen. They were first published in the *Irish Times* on the following dates:

Chapter One

i: 19 October 1940 ii: 17 March 1941 iii: 28 June 1941 iv: 15 August 1941 v: 15 August 1941 vi: 8 September 1941 vii: 12 September 1941 viii: 22 September 1941 ix: 24 September 1941 x: 24 September 1941 xi: 26 September 1941 xii: 10 October 1941 xiii: 22 October 1941 xiv: 27 October 1941 xv: 3 November 1941 xvi: 3 December 1941 xvii: 10 December 1941 xviii: 12 December 1941 xix: 15 December 1941 xx: 24 December 1941

Chapter Two

i: 27 July 1942 ii: 17 August 1942 iii: 17 August 1942 iv: 25 August 1942 v: 23 September 1942 vi: 28 September 1942 vii: 21 October 1942 viii: 9 November 1942 ix: 11 November 1942 x: 11 November 1942 xi: 11 December 1942 xii: 2 December 1942 xiii: 4 December 1942 xiv: 18 December 1942 xv: 9 January 1943 xvi: 11 January 1943 xvii: 16 January 1943

Chapter Three

i: 27 July 1942 ii: 17 August 1942 iii: 17 August 1942 iv: 25 August 1942 v: 23 September 1942 vi: 28 September 1942 vii: 21 October 1942 viii: 9 November 1942 ix: 2 December 1942 x: 4 December 1942 xi: 11 December 1942 xii: 11 December 1942 xiii: 16 December 1942 xiv: 18 December 1942 xv: 9 January 1943 xvi: 11 January 1943 xvii: 16 January 1943

Chapter Four

i: 25 January 1943 ii: 1 February 1943 iii: 15 February 1943 iv: 19 February 1943 v: 3 March 1943 vi: 11 March 1943 vii: 13 March

Acknowledgements and sources

1943 viii: 13 March 1943 ix: 19 March 1943 x: 16 April 1943 xi: 31 May 1943 xii: 21 July 1943 xiii: 21 July 1943 xiv: 28 July 1943 xv: 22 September 1943 xvi: 1 October 1943 xvii: 30 October 1943 xviii: 21 December 1943

Chapter Five

i: 27 January 1944 ii: 9 February 1944 iii: 28 February 1944 iv: 29 February 1944 v: 6 March 1944 vi: 16 March 1944 vii: 21 March 1944 viii: 22 March 1944 ix: 13 April 1944 x: 21 April 1944

Chapter Six

i: 21 August 1944 ii: 16 September 1944 iii: 20 September 1944 iv: 21 September 1944 v: 22 September 1944 vi: 22 September 1944 vii: 25 September 1944 viii: 2 October 1944 ix: 4 October 1944 x: 11 October 1944 xi: 23 October 1944 xii: 2 November 1944 xiii: 2 December 1944

Chapter Seven

i: 1 January 1945 ii: 9 January 1945 iii: 17 January 1945 iv: 7 February 1945 v: 26 April 1945 vi: 7 May 1945 vii: 1 June 1945 viii: 11 June 1945 ix: 26 June 1945 x: 3 July 1945 ix: 28 July 1945 xii: 4 August 1945

Chapter Eight

i: 20 August 1945 ii: 22 August 1945 iii: 1 September 1945 iv: 5 October 1945 v: 26 October 1945 vi: 27 October 1945 vii: 3 November 1945 viii: 14 November 1945 ix: 28 November 1945 x: 4 December 1945 xi: 20 December 1945 xii: 24 December 1945

Drawings by Hector McDonnell on pages 22, 47, 67, 70, 90, 92, 112, 114, 129, 132, 149, 152.

Cuttings by Flann O'Brien on pages 30, 35, 41, 45, 57, 100, 117, 118, 166, 167, 168.

LANNAN SELECTIONS

The Lannan Foundation, located in Santa Fe, New Mexico, is a family foundation whose funding focuses on special cultural projects and ideas which promote and protect cultural freedom, diversity, and creativity.

The literary aspect of Lannan's cultural program supports the creation and presentation of exceptional English-language literature and develops a wider audience for poetry, fiction, and nonfiction.

Since 1990, the Lannan Foundation has supported Dalkey Archive Press projects in a variety of ways, including monetary support for authors, audience development programs, and direct funding for the publication of the Press's books.

In the year 2000, the Lannan Selections Series was established to promote both organizations' commitment to the highest expressions of literary creativity. The Foundation supports the publication of this series of books each year, and works closely with the Press to ensure that these books will reach as many readers as possible and achieve a permanent place in literature. Authors whose works have been published as Lannan Selections include Ishmael Reed, Stanley Elkin, Ann Quin, Nicholas Mosley, William Eastlake, and David Antin, among others.

SELECTED DALKEY ARCHIVE PAPERBACKS

FOR A FULL LIST OF PUBLICATIONS, VISIT:
www.dalkeyarchive.com

⊒

SELECTED DALKEY ARCHIVE PAPERBACKS

To an Early Grave.
DAVID MARKSON, *Reader's Block.*
  Springer's Progress.
  Wittgenstein's Mistress.
CAROLE MASO, *AVA.*
LADISLAV MATEJKA AND KRYSTYNA POMORSKA, EDS.,
  Readings in Russian Poetics: Formalist and
  Structuralist Views.
HARRY MATHEWS,
  The Case of the Persevering Maltese: Collected Essays.
  Cigarettes.
  The Conversions.
  The Human Country: New and Collected Stories.
  The Journalist.
  Singular Pleasures.
  The Sinking of the Odradek Stadium.
  Tlooth.
  20 Lines a Day.
ROBERT L. MCLAUGHLIN, ED.,
  Innovations: An Anthology of Modern &
    Contemporary Fiction.
STEVEN MILLHAUSER, *The Barnum Museum.*
  In the Penny Arcade.
RALPH J. MILLS, JR., *Essays on Poetry.*
OLIVE MOORE, *Spleen.*
NICHOLAS MOSLEY, *Accident.*
  Assassins.
  Catastrophe Practice.
  Children of Darkness and Light.
  The Hesperides Tree.
  Hopeful Monsters.
  Imago Bird.
  Impossible Object.
  Inventing God.
  Judith.
  Natalie Natalia.
  Serpent.
  The Uses of Slime Mould: Essays of Four Decades.
WARREN F. MOTTE, JR.,
  Fables of the Novel: French Fiction since 1990.
  Oulipo: A Primer of Potential Literature.
YVES NAVARRE, *Our Share of Time.*
WILFRIDO D. NOLLEDO, *But for the Lovers.*
FLANN O'BRIEN, *At Swim-Two-Birds.*
  At War.
  The Best of Myles.
  The Dalkey Archive.
  Further Cuttings.
  The Hard Life.
  The Poor Mouth.
  The Third Policeman.
CLAUDE OLLIER, *The Mise-en-Scène.*
FERNANDO DEL PASO, *Palinuro of Mexico.*
ROBERT PINGET, *The Inquisitory.*
RAYMOND QUENEAU, *The Last Days.*
  Odile.
  Pierrot Mon Ami.
  Saint Glinglin.
ANN QUIN, *Berg.*
  Passages.
  Three.
  Tripticks.
ISHMAEL REED, *The Free-Lance Pallbearers.*
  The Last Days of Louisiana Red.
  Reckless Eyeballing.
  The Terrible Threes.

The Terrible Twos.
  Yellow Back Radio Broke-Down.
JULIÁN RÍOS, *Poundemonium.*
AUGUSTO ROA BASTOS, *I the Supreme.*
JACQUES ROUBAUD, *The Great Fire of London.*
  Hortense in Exile.
  Hortense Is Abducted.
  The Plurality of Worlds of Lewis.
  The Princess Hoppy.
  Some Thing Black.
LEON S. ROUDIEZ, *French Fiction Revisited.*
LUIS RAFAEL SÁNCHEZ, *Macho Camacho's Beat.*
SEVERO SARDUY, *Cobra & Maitreya.*
NATHALIE SARRAUTE, *Do You Hear Them?*
  Martereau.
ARNO SCHMIDT, *Collected Stories.*
  Nobodaddy's Children.
CHRISTINE SCHUTT, *Nightwork.*
GAIL SCOTT, *My Paris.*
JUNE AKERS SEESE,
  Is This What Other Women Feel Too?
  What Waiting Really Means.
AURELIE SHEEHAN, *Jack Kerouac Is Pregnant.*
VIKTOR SHKLOVSKY,
  A Sentimental Journey: Memoirs 1917-1922.
  Theory of Prose.
  Third Factory.
  Zoo, or Letters Not about Love.
JOSEF ŠKVORECKÝ,
  The Engineer of Human Souls.
CLAUDE SIMON, *The Invitation.*
GILBERT SORRENTINO, *Aberration of Starlight.*
  Blue Pastoral.
  Crystal Vision.
  Imaginative Qualities of Actual Things.
  Mulligan Stew.
  Pack of Lies.
  The Sky Changes.
  Something Said.
  Splendide-Hôtel.
  Steelwork.
  Under the Shadow.
W. M. SPACKMAN, *The Complete Fiction.*
GERTRUDE STEIN, *Lucy Church Amiably.*
  The Making of Americans.
  A Novel of Thank You.
PIOTR SZEWC, *Annihilation.*
ESTHER TUSQUETS, *Stranded.*
DUBRAVKA UGRESIC, *Thank You for Not Reading.*
LUISA VALENZUELA, *He Who Searches.*
BORIS VIAN, *Heartsnatcher.*
PAUL WEST, *Words for a Deaf Daughter & Gala.*
CURTIS WHITE, *Memories of My Father Watching TV.*
  Monstrous Possibility.
  Requiem.
DIANE WILLIAMS, *Excitability: Selected Stories.*
  Romancer Erector.
DOUGLAS WOOLF, *Wall to Wall.*
  Ya! & John-Juan.
PHILIP WYLIE, *Generation of Vipers.*
MARGUERITE YOUNG, *Angel in the Forest.*
  Miss MacIntosh, My Darling.
REYOUNG, *Unbabbling.*
LOUIS ZUKOFSKY, *Collected Fiction.*
SCOTT ZWIREN, *God Head.*

FOR A FULL LIST OF PUBLICATIONS, VISIT:
www.dalkeyarchive.com